Fifty Shades of Grace

Love Changes Everything

NICHOLAS J. DEERE

ISBN 978-1512385755

Table of Contents

INTRODUCTION:
Unspoken Memories

Some memories are too precious to be spoken out loud; doing so might shatter the special place they hold in our hearts. But some memories are too precious *not* to be spoken out loud, when doing so might bring hope and healing to the hearts of those who hear them.

Memories are powerful things. They can stick with you for life, like this one shared by a character named Mr. Bernstein in the movie *Citizen Kane*. A reporter had asked Mr. Bernstein how Charles Kane could have possibly remembered a fleeting moment with a girl from so many years earlier. Mr. Bernstein replied:

"You're pretty young, Mr. Thompson. A fellow will remember a lot of things you wouldn't think he'd remember. You take me. One day, back in 1896, I was crossing over to Jersey on the ferry, and as we pulled out, there was another ferry pulling in, and on it there was a girl waiting to get off. A white dress she had on. She was carrying a white parasol. I only saw her for one second. She didn't see me at all, but I'll bet a month hasn't gone by since that I haven't thought of that girl."

You probably have memories like these. I know I do. This book is full of them.

I've never shared most of these memories with anyone, and I'm hesitant to share them with you now. It's not because I don't want you to know about them (well, there's a little bit of that), but it's because they are so personal to me, so intimate, that I'm afraid by sharing them they might somehow shatter.

I'm afraid to share them because I would hate to have someone take them lightly or laugh at them (although some of them *are* light and laughable). I'm afraid to share them because of what someone might think of me. I wonder if they would still love me the same if they really knew some of my innermost thoughts. I'm afraid to share them because some of them are truly embarrassing—I can't believe I thought and did some of the things I share in this book.

At the same time, I believe that some of these memories could be very helpful (extremely helpful, in fact), especially for anyone who has pondered any of the thoughts and feelings that I share here. I remember walking through "the stacks" in the graduate library at the University of Illinois when I was a freshman. As an underclassman, I had to get special permission to go into those rows upon rows of books housed in room after room of that massive library. But I had a mission. I wanted (I needed) to find out what other people thought about some of the things I was grappling with in my mind.

There was no Internet back then; nowhere to quickly look up the topics that were burning on my heart. I was excited to find that at least a few books were listed in the card catalog on these subjects. But after getting permission to enter the stacks, I was disappointed to find that the books on these topics took up a mere five or six inches of shelf space out of the hundreds of shelves that filled that one room. I thumbed through each of those books, but found them to be clinical and dry, doing little to help me with my practical questions.

I wish I had held this book in my hands back then. I think I would have been amazed to find that someone else had the same thoughts and experiences I was having. I would have loved to learn from them as much as I could, whether I agreed with their conclusions or not. I just wished someone would have shared their thoughts and memories with me.

So after all these years of gathering and storing these precious memories in my mind, I'd like to pull them out and share them with you. My hope is that you'll be able to benefit from them in a special way.

Before you dive into this book, however, I want to give you a fair warning. This *is* a love story. If you're not interested in reading about passion and romance, heartbreak and sex (or staying up late to find out what's next), then this isn't the book for you.

If, on the other hand, you'd like to explore and experience a life lived in love, with all of its glorious, unpredictable and multi-faceted dimensions, then read on. It's for you that I've shared these "unspoken memories."

Nicholas J. Deere
May 25, 2015

P.S. The memories I share in this book are all true;
Just the names have been changed (including mine, too).
When choosing a pen name I even mulled over
Names like Laurel or Mary (or Debbie Macomber?),
'Cause who wants to read romance that's been penned by a guy?
But if Shakespeare could do it... (then I guess so can I!).

PART 1 ~ DIVING IN

Chapter 1:

Turkish Delight

We were just kids. Seven, maybe eight years old. Two boys just messing around. My friend and I were playing in my parents' bedroom when we discovered my mom's jewelry drawer, so we started trying on her rings and bracelets. My friend found her lipstick and put some on his lips. We laughed. I put some on mine and we laughed again.

The next thing I knew we were rolling around on the bed, kissing and laughing and getting lipstick all over our faces. It was a total blast. I had kissed a boy, and I liked it.

A few years later we were in junior high. I was sleeping over at his house one night after a club meeting. He fell asleep in the bed next to mine, but I couldn't sleep. As I looked at him lying there on the bed, I wondered what it would be like to kiss him again. I wondered if he would remember we had kissed before. I wondered if I should wake him up and see.

But I was too nervous to find out. I rolled back over in my bed and finally fell asleep. I never did mention it to him.

Things were different now, though. Now I was in college and living on my own. I was spending the summer on campus between my freshman and sophomore years at the University of Illinois. I worked on the grounds crew during the day, mowing the quad, picking up litter and weeding the flower beds at the base of the Alma Mater, a motherly statue that welcomed students to the school from all over the world.

One of those students that she welcomed was my new friend Mathieu. He had come to the U of I from overseas, and we became friends during my freshman year in the dorms. My parents had always hosted international friends and students at our farm a few hours away, and I had traveled enough by then myself to know how hard it was to be a stranger in a strange land. So I went out of my way to make friends with Mathieu. We hung out after work, going for pizza at Garcia's or walking and talking on the quad.

One afternoon, when we were hanging out at his place, he got up to get something off the shelf across the room. As he walked past me, I couldn't help but notice how nice his khaki pants fit on him. They looked soft and smooth and snug in all the right places. *I wish mine fit like that*, I thought.

But my next thought went beyond just thinking about how nice his pants *looked* on him. I wondered how they would *feel* on him. I thought it would be so easy to reach out and touch them with my hands, running my fingers over the smooth cloth, feeling the folds of the material as it disappeared around the curve of his bottom. I could never do it, of course. I could never reach out and touch another man like that. But the thought did run through my mind. *I wish I had pants that fit like that*, I thought again.

The next day, Mathieu came over to my house after work. I was living with an elderly woman, a long-time friend of the family whose father had taught at the university many years before. She was still active in a variety of campus events, so she was gone from the house much of the time. She was gone again that night when Mathieu came over to hang out with me.

As we sat on the front porch, a screened-in entryway to the house which was secluded by plants and vines that grew up and over the wide-arching windows, Mathieu opened up and shared with me a painful story from his past. When he was young, he was raped by two women. He said he knew it must sound odd for a man to be raped by two women. But against his will they had touched him, aroused him and forced themselves on him.

He hesitated frequently as he told me the story. I could see it had impacted him deeply, so I listened quietly and let him talk. He went on to tell me that this experience had affected his view of women, particularly in regards to how he viewed them sexually.

I felt sorry for him and for the impact it had upon him. Having never had a sexual encounter myself at that point, I could only imagine what he must have experienced. The net effect on him, he said, was that he felt uncomfortable around women sexually. He said he actually felt more comfortable around men.

The more we talked, the more I was able to share with him my own discomfort at the idea of having sex with a woman, not because of any negative experience I had with women like he had shared, but because I always wanted to treat women with the utmost dignity and respect. I had many close friends who were girls when I was growing up, and hearing the way they talked about the guys they dated, I never wanted to be like one of *them*. So I always tried to treat women with gentleness and respect. I kept my eyes in contact with theirs whenever I could, never letting my eyes glance down below their neck, even if I wanted to take a look. I went out of my way to make sure women knew I wasn't interested in doing any of the things that other men did with them. In so doing, I became a "safe" friend for many women. They shared their personal thoughts with me, and I was glad for their confidence.

Men, on the other hand, were more of a mystery. Although I had a few close guy friends growing up, I wasn't friends with a lot of the "manly man" types of guys at our school. I had never seriously considered homosexuality as an alternative to having sex with a woman, other than a few fleeting moments, like the time I spent the night at my friend's house in junior high. But that didn't keep other guys at school from thinking I was gay. They said I was always hanging around with girls, but not the way they hung out with girls.

It didn't help that I loved doing things like singing and dancing, playing the piano and the flute and doing gymnastics. In a town where most of the guys played football or basketball or wrestled each other to the ground, I was pretty much out of step. I had a high sensitivity to pain, and I never liked contact sports because of it. This alienated me, of course, even further from the guys all around me. I played in the marching band, sang in the choir and took dance and gymnastics at a bigger town nearby. When the guys called me a faggot or said that I must be gay, I had to look up the words in the dictionary because I didn't even know what they were talking about. I was just doing things I loved to do. I never thought of myself as gay, and I was hurt and bummed that they thought I was. I wished they could have liked me and appreciated me for who I was.

Why did I love doing those things? I played the piano because everyone in my family played the piano, from my brother and sister, to my mom and dad, to my grandma and grandpa. I played the flute and did gymnastics because a man from Switzerland came to visit us at the farm one day. He pulled out a flute that he said he played when he went on long walks through the Swiss Alps. And when he walked on his hands across our living room floor, I thought that was the coolest thing ever. So when I had a chance to be in the band at school and pick out an instrument, I picked out the flute. When my sister took gymnastics and I went along for the ride, I asked my mom if I could take lessons and learn how to walk on my hands, too! I didn't think there was anything gay or girlish about these things, because I had learned about playing the flute and doing gymnastics from one of the manliest "mountain men" I had ever met.

I was also in no way averse to women. I remember holding hands and cuddling up next to my first sweetheart in fourth grade after ice skating around the pond in town. I shared a kiss with another girl a few years later after riding bikes for miles and miles around the country roads near our farm. I dated another girl in high school and loved kissing her lips while sitting on the living room floor at her house in front of the fireplace. (But when we tried to french kiss one day after hearing our friends talk about it, I felt we had crossed a line that we shouldn't have crossed. I didn't know why, but it felt like we were going too far, so we retreated back to holding hands and friendly kisses.) Being physically close to her felt so good and I loved spending time with her, but we eventually broke up and went our separate ways after high school. When I went to college, I even met a few women that first year and thought, *Wow! I'd love to marry her...or her...or her!*

But now, here I was with Mathieu, a man who, for the first time in my life, seemed to truly appreciate my gifts and my talents, from music and dance to drama and gymnastics. As he shared his aversion to women and his interest in men, I realized he might be interested in more with me, too. I couldn't believe it! Just the day before, as he had walked past me on his way to the bookshelf, I wondered what it would be like to reach out and touch him, to feel the folds of his khaki pants as they curved around his bottom.

The more we talked, the more I realized I was facing a dilemma I had never faced before. When he finally asked me what I thought about everything he had just said, I couldn't hold back from telling him the truth. I told him what I had thought when he walked past me the day before, that I wondered what it would be like to touch another man—to touch him. He asked me if I'd like to find out.

I couldn't imagine there would ever be a better opportunity. We were all alone, we had nothing but time on our hands and we were already sharing some of the most intimate moments of our lives with each other.

We began to touch each other in ways that I had never

touched, or been touched by anyone else before, whether male or female. We were fully aroused, just touching each other with our hands. Although we never had full sexual intercourse, we definitely brought each other to a full and mutually agreeable climax. And it felt good. Really good. I had kissed a man, and I liked it.

I felt like Edmund must have felt in the *Chronicles of Narnia* books when the White Witch gave him his first taste of Turkish delight. I had never tasted anything more delicious. And I just wanted more and more and more.

Chapter 2:
Golden Bubble

That was the best summer of my life (at least up to that point). To find a man who loved me, cared about me and wanted to share his life with me in the way that he did went beyond any friendship I had ever had. We talked and hiked, played tennis and rode bikes, went to movies, went to dinner and went to bed. I loved it all.

Although Mathieu and I had other friends we hung out with on campus that summer, we kept the sexual side of our friendship a secret, adding all the more to its intrigue and excitement. We would go to work during the day at our respective jobs, then hang out as much as possible at night, doing anything and everything we wanted. As far as we knew, no one suspected we were anything other than good friends, which we were—*really, really* good friends.

So it was hard when the fall came and I had to leave him behind. At the end of the previous semester, I had signed up for a study abroad program in Salzburg, Austria. I was going there to study Austrian history, culture and economics as part of my business training for the U of I. Although I knew I would miss seeing Mathieu every day, he had opened up a whole new world to me that I had never known before.

When I got to Austria, I bought a Eurail pass so I could take the trains anywhere in Europe, at any time, at no extra cost. So I traveled on weekends as much as I could to see the countries nearby: Germany, Switzerland, France, Italy. I loved taking it all in.

One of my new friends at the school, Lee, suggested we should go to Greece during our fall break. I thought it sounded awesome. I met Lee my first day in Europe when our whole school (it was pretty small!) started the school year by taking a bus tour through Germany down the Rhein River. The director of the school was an art aficionado, so she always started the school year with this tour of the many cathedrals, castles and museums along the Rhein. The trip gave us all a chance to get to know each other and to get to know the art and culture of the surrounding area.

Lee was my roommate on the first night of that tour. Partway through the night, Lee rolled over and put his arm around me, saying "Oh, Gary." It was a little awkward, but I let it ride since he was still sleeping. The next morning on the bus, we were all laughing about the night before; some people had roommates who snored, some had roommates who took all the blankets and I mentioned that Lee put his arm around me while he was sleeping and said, "Oh, Gary."

He said, "I must have been dreaming about my friend back home, Carey. She's one of my best friends." We all laughed, and I never thought anything more about it. At least, not until our trip to Greece.

We bought our plane tickets and flew to the island of Crete, out in the middle of the Mediterranean Sea, not knowing anyone or anything about the country. I didn't, anyway. Lee, however, as I discovered as our trip progressed, knew just where he wanted to go.

On our first day out, he suggested we go see an X-rated movie. I had never seen an X-rated movie before, but I thought, *Why not?* I had hardly ever seen any R-rated movies for that matter, other than Brooke Shields in *Blue Lagoon*. This was no *Blue Lagoon*.

The next day, we headed to a blue lagoon of our own, ending up at a place called Matala Bay. It was a secluded beach on the south shore of Crete, and I had never seen such a striking shoreline. Yellow sandstone cliffs jutted out into the deep blue water of the Mediterranean. I watched with fascination as people jumped into the water from a thirty-foot cliff on the other side of the bay. We were sitting at a beachside café with some friends from our school that we had run into, and I was enjoying a gin and tonic and my first taste of fried calamari (squid). One of the girls said she liked how they tasted, except for the fact that the testicles kept getting stuck to the inside of her mouth. We laughed so hard, because she meant to say "tentacles." We thought that was a Freudian slip if there ever was one (when you say one thing, but you mean your mother).

As we kept watching these guys jump into the water, I said, "I want to try that, too!" A man sitting at the table next to us said he could show me where to jump so I wouldn't hit the rocks below. I wasn't sure if I should be *comforted* by those words or *terrified* by them, but I still wanted to do it. So after lunch we swam out to the base of the cliffs, climbed up and over the rocks until we were finally standing at the top of the cliff, looking out over the edge.

I had never been so scared in my life. From that vantage point, I could see the two huge boulders he was talking about that were just beneath the surface of the water below, one on the right and one on the left of the spot where I was supposed to jump. But my new friend (whom I had just met at the table next to us) took the first jump and he survived, so I was determined to do it, too. I backed up a few steps against the cliff wall behind me, held my breath, then bounded forward, pushing off the edge of the cliff and leaping as far away as I could so I wouldn't hit the face of the cliff on the way down.

The free fall was such a rush that it was only when I was about to hit the water below that I realized I needed to take another breath. Too late! Just as I opened my mouth to take that breath, my feet, my privates and all the rest of my body slammed into the water. I sank down, feeling like my whole body had been smacked by a board. But when I popped my head back up above the water, I gave the "thumbs up" to the others and said I couldn't wait to do it again! Man, this was living!

Later that day, my friend Lee and I hiked around the cliffs where we had been jumping, walking several miles away along the water's edge. Finding a cache of red clay near the shore, which was native to that area and from which much of the local pottery was made, we decided to turn the clay into a spa treatment. We slipped off our swimsuits, covered ourselves in clay and laid out on the warm yellow sandstone. I never mentioned to my friend that I had been in a gay relationship, and he never mentioned he had either. We just laid there, covered in a thin layer of clay, enjoying the sun. What a way to spend the day, half a world away from where I grew up! I had never been so far from home in my life—in more ways than one.

After touring some more of Crete and seeing the land of the ancient minotaur from Greek mythology, Lee and I took an overnight boat from the north side of the island to Athens, the capitol of Greece on the mainland. We climbed to the top of the Acropolis and stood amazed as we looked up at those towering pillars which once made up the Parthenon. After touring Athens, Lee said he'd like to see one more island before we left Greece. We looked at some brochures at a local travel stand and saw many interesting islands, but Lee wanted to go to one in particular: Mykonos.

So we jumped on a high-speed boat run by a local tour company and darted off for a five-hour ride to this remote island. By that evening, we were walking through the narrow streets of Mykonos, bounded on each side by Mediterranean villas, all of which looked like they belonged in the Mediterranean (surprise!) with their classic white walls and flat roofs.

We visited a few clubs for a bite here and a drink there, ending up at a dance club where Lee looked like he was in heaven. He loved to dance, and he was extremely good looking, so for every song he had a partner—not all of whom were women.

As the night rolled on, it became more and more apparent to me that Mykonos wasn't just any island; it was a haven for gays and lesbians. Lee and I were ripe targets for many gazing eyes, much to Lee's delight, and even to my own curiosity and fascination.

We didn't have a place to stay for the night because Lee said he was sure he could find us a place easy enough. He was right. Well after midnight, he told me he'd found us a place to stay— right upstairs from the club. He had made friends with the two gay club owners who happily invited us upstairs to spend the night with them.

When the club shut down for the night, the owners led us to their place upstairs. It looked like a movie set. We walked into a room filled with Greek statues, lush paintings and rich fabrics. A nude statue here and an erotic painting there only added to the already exotic appeal. After another drink and a brief chat, it was time for bed. I figured I'd be spending the night with Lee, but I was surprised when one of the owners took Lee into one room and the other owner took me into his.

There was only one bed in this owner's beautifully appointed room, which he said I could share with him. For a twenty-year-old farm boy from the heartland of America, this was somewhere between totally exhilarating and downright freaky. As we turned out the lights, I laid awake with my heart beating fast, trying to take in all that had happened during the day. I was still in shock from the realization that Lee must be gay. Then all of a sudden, the owner of the club rolled over in the bed towards me, putting his hand on my thigh.

My fascination about everything turned to panic. Here I

was, on an island in a faraway corner of the Mediterranean, in a bed with a man I had just met some twenty minutes earlier. What was I thinking? What was I doing? What was Lee thinking? And what was Lee *doing,* right now, with the other owner of the club in the other room?!?

Lee never told me he was gay! He never told me that he knew Mykonos was a well-known hot spot for gays! He never told me when we came to this remote island that his plan all along was to pick up a man and spend the night with him!

As all of these thoughts burst into my head, I panicked. My fear of just a few days before, standing at the edge of a cliff before jumping into the water thirty feet below, was nothing compared to the fear I felt now. What would this man laying next to me do to me if I said, "Yes"? And perhaps even scarier, what would he do to me if I said, "No"?

As the owner began to move his hand up my thigh, I knew I had to decide fast. There was no time to lose. I reached over and touched his hand. Then, as politely as I could, I said, "Thank you, but, no, thank you," and I moved his hand off my thigh. Without another word, he rolled over onto his side of the bed again. A little while later, he got up and left. The following morning I learned that he had joined Lee and the other owner for a menage à trois of their own.

As for me, I was so thankful and relieved that I had resisted his advance. As eager as I was to visit Greece with all its exotic delights, I was now even more eager to leave.

I felt like Monica Lewinsky must have felt when she was in the midst of her infamous affair with the president of the United States. For her it was thrilling and dangerous, all at the same time. In speaking about her affair in her first major public address sixteen years later, Monica said she deeply regretted what she had done for many reasons, not the least of which was that people got hurt. But she described those two secret years of her life as the "golden bubble" part of her story. "It was my everything," she said.

Her bubble burst, however, when the affair became public one day, and she was shamed and humiliated by people—and nations—around the world within twenty-four hours.

For me, my trip to Greece was still in the beginning days of my own two-year "golden bubble." But I was already starting to realize that if I kept daring life, playing around at its edges, that my bubble could burst at any time, too. It hadn't burst yet, though. And, to be honest, I was enthralled by the whole adventure of it, the glamour of it and the exhilaration of it—even the parts that scared me to death.

I had never felt so alive in my life!

Chapter 3:
Missing Cookies

When Lee and I flew back to Salzburg, our conversations took a new turn as we both realized we were mutually interested in all things homosexual. It also turned out that when he had put his arm around me that first night on the bus trip through Germany, saying, "Oh, Gary," he really *did* have a boyfriend back home named Gary. (He also had a girl friend he knew named Carey, but that's not who he had been thinking of that night!)

We traveled together again over the next few weekends with a few other friends from school to Venice and Florence, where we rode gondolas on the canals, twirled spaghetti on our spoons and stared at Michelangelo's immense, naked statue of *David*—perhaps a little longer than we should have.

Our travels eventually led us to the city of Vienna, where a much larger group from our school was going to take in more Austrian art, music and apple strudel. One rainy afternoon in Vienna, Lee asked if I wanted to stay back at the hotel while the rest of the group went out to explore the city.

Lee and I seemed to be getting closer and closer since our trip to Greece. So I wasn't surprised, and I was truly complimented, when he asked me if I wanted to stay back with him at the hotel. I knew what he wanted. We went up to our room and began to undress each other.

It felt so good to be touched. When I went to kiss his lips, he held his finger up to his mouth to indicate that I shouldn't. We could do other things, he said, but not that. Unsure why he wouldn't want me to kiss him, but would let me do other things with him sexually, I skipped over that oddity and we proceeded to enjoy each other in other ways until we were both mutually satisfied. (I found out later that he had an oral venereal disease which he didn't want to pass on to me, and for which I was ever-so thankful that he didn't let me kiss him!)

As I lay there in the afterglow of getting to be so close to this man who was so attractive to me and to so many others, I heard a key in the lock at the door. We had two other roommates in our room that weekend—and one of them was coming in!

Startled, we rolled to opposite sides of the bed, pulling the covers over our naked bodies, with our clothes lying on the floor, as if our roommate would somehow think we were just taking an afternoon nap. After an awkward exchange of hellos, none of us knew what to say next. In fact, from that point on, my friend Lee, with whom I had spent so many colorful weekends, ignored me almost completely.

I was crushed. How could we have been getting so close to each other, even to the point of being sexually intimate, only to have *all* kindness and conversation—or even friendliness, for that matter—shut down? It wasn't until I was playing the piano at our school one day, rehearsing with a group for a song we were going to do at a Christmas party later in the week, that I heard Lee mention anything about the incident again.

As I was playing the piano, the roommate who walked in on us in Vienna referred to me as "Little Amadeus." We were living in Salzburg—the birthplace of the famous pianist Wolfgang Amadeus Mozart—so I looked up and smiled appreciatively at his comment. When I smiled, though, Lee said, "Look, he thinks it's a compliment!"

I had no idea what he was talking about. If it wasn't a compliment, what was it? It wasn't until later that I learned they were referring to a play they had both seen called *Amadeus*, (later made into a movie) in which Mozart was portrayed as a sexual deviant, frequently indulging in various sexcapades, even at a very young age. I was heartbroken. My friends weren't complimenting me on my piano playing—something which was so precious to me—they were comparing me to a sexual misfit.

When it came time for the Christmas party—which was being held next door to our school in the mansion used for the filming of the movie *The Sound of Music*—I couldn't believe I was getting to play the piano at this famous home that was used to film all those scenes from a movie I had watched since childhood. (Our school actually met in the old, but well-maintained stable buildings on the grounds of that estate, with a view of the gazebo from the movie and the Untersberg Mountain off in the distance across the lake. It was remarkable!) Yet I couldn't shake the disturbing feeling I had inside me that my friendship with Lee had fallen apart ever since our intimate afternoon in Vienna. Fear and guilt had free reign in my mind.

After the Christmas party, and with my emotions still vacillating between the highs and lows of the week, another guy from our school, Taylor, approached me for the first time, wondering if I would be interested in a sexual encounter with him. Whether he had heard about my experience in Vienna with Lee or decided to test the waters of his own accord, I had no idea. But in the midst of my own hurt and frustration, I decided to take him up on his offer.

In the remaining days before the semester was over, I had a few more intimate encounters with Taylor. Each time, however, I felt worse and worse about what I was doing, and each time I wondered why it wasn't making me feel any better about the broken friendship I was experiencing with Lee. I was feeling even farther from home than ever, and I was looking forward to getting back.

Before I left for the airport, Taylor met me and handed me

a tasteful, but nude photograph of himself that he had taken for an art project for school. On the back he had written, "Don't cry because it's over. Smile because it was beautiful." He said that the mother of the Austrian host family where he was staying had told him that phrase that morning at breakfast, because he was crying so hard that I was leaving. Although I felt I had invested so little in our relationship, apparently he felt he had invested much more. When I got back to the United States, I found out there were more tears to come, but not from Taylor.

When I got home, I was so happy to finally see Mathieu again, a true friend from the summer before and with whom I had exchanged so many letters during that semester apart. I was eager to share everything with him in person that had happened on the trip because we had shared so much about our intimate lives before.

For some reason, though, he wasn't reacting the same way he had reacted before. When I described the details of my trip to Greece and the other exotic places I had visited and encounters that I had, rather than being excited for me, he was hurt. *How could he not be happy for me,* I wondered, *when he was the one who had opened up this whole new side of life for me?* Why wasn't he ecstatic that I was now exploring it even more? Somehow I didn't put two and two together, that the same hurt that I had felt when Lee suddenly stopped talking to me was minuscule compared to the hurt—and betrayal—Mathieu was feeling, knowing that I had been with other men while we were apart.

Mathieu finally shared with me the depth of his hurt. It went beyond the betrayal of our friendship he had felt when I had so casually mentioned my other sexual experiences. He had come to realize that it would probably never work out for us to spend the rest of our lives together.

Inwardly, when our relationship was first starting to bloom and take shape, he had hoped that we might one day move to some cosmopolitan city on the far side of the world where no one else knew us, and we could live out our lives as a gay couple.

But the more he talked to me, the more he could tell that this wasn't my plan for our relationship. I had no plans at all, in fact. While I was truly interested in continuing our really good friendship, and even our really good physical intimacy, he didn't feel he could do it, not knowing if we would ever spend the rest of our lives together.

As a good friend of his, I shouldn't have been surprised by his deep desire to be with me forever. But I was. Everything was still so new to me that I hadn't begun to wonder about the lifelong implications of what I was doing. He, however, had been thinking about a relationship like this for years.

What had started with so much excitement and intrigue was now turning out to deliver nothing but pain and heartbreak. After three forays now into the world of homosexual relationships, I was already starting to feel like my golden bubble was bursting.

I felt like Luke Skywalker in a frame of a comic strip where Darth Vader invited Luke to join him on the dark side. Darth said, "We have cookies!" so Luke agreed to join him. But in the next frame, Darth said (to a groaning Luke):

"Welcome to the Dark Side. Are you surprised we lied about the cookies?"

I was feeling like Luke, wondering, *What happened to the cookies?* When I started into homosexuality, I thought this might be a way to help meet my emotional and relational needs, and to get closer to other guys. But I was discovering—like so many others have discovered, whether male or female—that using sex to try to win someone else's heart can often end up *destroying* a bond of friendship rather than *sealing* it.

Chapter 4:

Wrong Places

In the spring, after I came back to the U of I from Salzburg, I decided to join a fraternity. I "rushed" at a few of the fraternity houses during "rush week," taking tours of the houses and meeting the guys who lived there. It was a chance for me to get to know them, and for them to get to know me, to see if we were a good fit for each other.

The idea of living with a houseful of guys sounded awesome to me, not because of the sexual possibilities of a living arrangement like that, but because I hoped it might make up for the lack of camaraderie and fun that I felt I had missed with other guys during my grade school and high school years.

Like many men who have homosexual attractions, I never had trouble relating to women. In fact, women were some of my best friends. My trouble was relating to men. My desire to hang out with men seemed to stem from a healthy need that all of us have for good, solid friendships with people of the same sex. As I was beginning to learn, sex with another man wasn't as important to me as a good, solid friendship. In fact, sex and romance seemed to get more in the way of just such a friendship.

All to say, I was really looking forward to the idea of joining a fraternity. One of the fraternities I checked out was one where a former roommate from the dorms had joined. I was glad when I got to his house, as I was greeted not only by my former roommate, but also by several of his friends, most of whom I had met during our semester together in the dorms.

The guys were all interested in talking to me, asking me all kinds of questions about my life and travels and interests. It felt good to have them so eager to talk to me. In fact, they talked to me so long, I didn't have a chance to tour the rest of the house or to meet any of the other guys who lived there.

The next day, someone from each house was designated to call back all the guys they wanted to invite for a second visit. A callback meant you could visit the house again, meet some more guys, and after that they would take a final vote on whether to let you move in or not. If you didn't get a call back, that meant they had already voted you down.

So the next morning when I woke up, I started getting ready for the callbacks. I wasn't sure how many of the houses would call me back, but I knew that at least my former roommate's house would call me back, as the interview had gone so well. I waited by the phone for an hour, then two, then three, but no one called. Finally, after four hours, I called my former roommate to see if they had forgotten to call. (Someone told me that happened sometimes, with so many people coming through. So I assumed that must have been the case here.)

My roommate didn't answer, so I called another friend. No answer there either. Finally, I got hold of another guy in the house and asked if there had been a problem. I heard the worst news a guy like me could hear: the house had "bonged" me and had voted me down. "Sorry," he said.

I later learned that my former roommate and his friends came to greet me at the door the night before because they didn't want anyone *else* in the house to meet me. That way, when the vote came up, they could all vote against me and keep me out.

I was crushed—again. All my confidence, my masculinity and my hopes for the coming semester were dashed in those moments of learning what had happened.

One house did call me back later in the day, however: the

house that was rumored as having the most gay members. It wasn't the house full of "blokes" that I had pictured. And some of the guys in that house even warned me (kiddingly, I hoped) not to drop my soap in the shower because of what might happen when I bent over to pick it up. So much for the boost in my masculinity.

Still, I was glad that *someone* wanted me, and some of the guys seemed like they could become really good friends. Since I was going to stay on campus during the summer to work on the grounds crew again, the guys in the house let me move in for summer break. There were only a few of us going to be living in the house that summer, holding the fort until everyone else returned in the fall.

I liked having almost the whole house to myself, taking over room #2 in a quiet corner. From time to time, some of the guys who were out of town that summer would drop in and hang out for a day or two.

One particular day, one of the nicest guys in the fraternity, Sean, came to visit the house. He was staying in town for just one night, and we spent the afternoon talking about all kinds of topics, including sex and homosexuality. As the day turned into night and it was time to go to bed, I told him he could stay with me in my room if he wanted. I had told him earlier in the day that I had fun sleeping next to people when I was traveling in Europe, even when there was nothing sexual between us. Sometimes four or five of us would take an afternoon break in the same bed and just hang out together. It was nice to be close to each other.

Sean said that sounded awesome to him, too, and why not? There was no one else around. We threw a futon mattress and a couple of pillows on the floor, then laid down to go to sleep. I asked if he cared if I put my arm around his shoulder because it was so comfortable and peaceful when I did that with others in the past. He thought that sounded great, too.

After feeling rejected by guys in my life, both intentionally and unintentionally, it was nice to have Sean's affirmation and acceptance. He seemed to really understand some of my innermost feelings (and it didn't hurt that he was popular and extremely good looking, having modeled for various campus publications). Having his affirmation was like having some of his popularity and good looks rub off on me, too.

I was so thankful that I just laid there for ten or fifteen minutes with my eyes closed, enjoying the moment. I couldn't fall asleep, though, and when I opened my eyes again, I saw that Sean still had his eyes open, too. He was just laying there looking at me. What started as a simple arm around his shoulder gravitated towards something more. Neither of us could sleep, it turned out, and neither of us wanted to resist the heightened sexuality we felt from lying there so close to each other. When we *did* finally fall asleep that night, it was only after gratifying ourselves by intimately touching each other —which was what both of us had privately *hoped* would be the outcome of our evening.

When I woke up the next morning, Sean was still sleeping next to me, laying there like a Greek god in all his slender but statuesque glory. He eventually woke up and went out to run an errand for an hour or so. To my surprise, he came back with a bunch of packaged flowers and a vinyl album of Stevie Wonder singing "Send One Your Love," (which says, in part: *"Show him your love, don't hold back your feelings, you don't need a reason, when it's straight from the heart"*). I was totally caught off guard by his heartfelt display of emotion. It was only then that he told me that this was the first time he had ever slept with a man. While he had thought about it and dreamed about it before, he had never actually done it. My invitation for him to sleep next to me was just what he needed to usher him into the evocative world of homosexuality.

I was stunned. I had no idea this was his first time. I

thought *I* was the newcomer to this party—especially with him. Yet there he was, profusely thankful for this new experience, one of the best, he said, of his entire life. Up to that point, others had always been the ones who invited me into sexual encounters. Now, although unbeknownst to me, I realized that I was the one who was doing the inviting.

Sean went home later that day, and although we continued to talk and hang out in the months ahead, we never had another encounter like that again. I had opened the door for him, and he was happy to walk through it on his own.

That fall, I found myself opening the door to homosexuality for another friend from the fraternity, too.

Reed was in my pledge class and we connected on several levels. We loved talking about life, love and travel. He was intrigued by my penchant for exploring new things, and he wanted to try whatever I had tried. He even signed up to study abroad in Salzburg the following January. When he said he'd like to try out homosexuality, I wasn't surprised—and I was happy to oblige. I was thankful he felt our friendship had become so close.

At Christmastime, he asked if I'd like to go skiing with him in the Swiss Alps before his classes started in Salzburg. He said he'd pay for everything. He knew I loved to travel and probably wouldn't say no. He was right. Having grown up in a small town in Illinois where some of my friends had never traveled out of the state, let alone out of the country, I was thrilled to be off on yet another adventure. And this time it would be on an all-expense-paid trip to the Swiss Alps, where no one would know us and we could do whatever we wanted. It sounded like the ultimate freedom.

Reed flew over ahead of me and I flew over the day after Christmas. We were going to meet at one of the several different hotels he had booked for our trip. As I was riding in the taxi from the airport to our first hotel, I couldn't help but feel this was all so adventurous, so secretive.

When I arrived at the hotel, I went up to meet him, as he had given me the room number. But on my way to the room, when I realized where I was going, I thought he might have overdone it. He had reserved a top-floor, penthouse suite. Even though I was glad to see him when I opened the door, I felt incredibly awkward by everything he had done in preparation for our first night there.

He had lit candles all around the room and laid out Christmas presents for me on the bed. Water was steaming up from the hot tub in the adjacent room and starting to foam with the bubbles he had poured in. This wasn't what I had pictured at all! I was picturing two blokes heading out to the mountains to ski! This was something you would do with your wife on your wedding night, if you could ever afford such a thing! It was all too sensual, too romantic. To top it all off, he had dyed his hair a flaming color the day before. The scarf he was wearing around his neck was just as flaming as his hair! I freaked out more than a little bit, and I let him know it.

At the same time, it was hard *not* to be thankful for his genuine display of care and attention—however excessive it may have been. He knew what I liked from all of our previous conversations, and he had bought me gifts that were very personal and meaningful to me. But why did it all have to be so, well, gay? Was this really what I wanted for my life, and from my relationships with guys? My head was spinning again with emotions.

Thankfully we were in a country where no one knew us, and even though I felt more conspicuous than ever that we were a "couple" wherever we went, I decided to take it for what it was—even if it wasn't what I had expected it to be. And we did get to go skiing in the Swiss Alps on New Year's Eve, ringing in the New Year with champagne and a phenomenal meal at yet another exclusive hotel.

At the end of the week, we learned that the last hotel where we were staying took only cash—no credit cards and no checks. I found out that day that my friend wasn't actually paying for our trip. Reed was using his dad's credit card, his dad whom he despised and hated in every way. This trip was, in part, yet another way for my friend to spit in his dad's face, for he felt like his dad had never accepted him nor understood his sensitive nature. I began to see that this trip wasn't just about the care I knew he genuinely felt for me, but also about his rebellion against everything that he felt had constrained him in the past. I happened to come along when he was ready to vent his frustration to the full, leaving his old world behind for good and entering into a world that was totally new and different.

Although I still cared about Reed, and he seemed to care about me, I was disappointed again. Like my friend, Sean, who earlier in the summer had given me flowers and his favorite album, Reed also thanked me profusely for bringing him into this new way of living. I was having an influence on people around me, but I wasn't sure if it was entirely good, if it was good at all. When Reed finally got to Salzburg the first week of school, he decided it was too bland for his newfound tastes. He dropped out of that school and moved to another country to attend another school that was more progressive and more in line with his emerging lifestyle.

When I got back to the States, I found myself on the receiving end of an irate phone call from Reed's father. He exploded with rage, wondering how his son could have spent all that money—*his* money. What was he thinking? And had I spend that much on the trip, too? I couldn't even reply. I got a glimpse that day of the anger that was burning inside Reed's father; but I have to say Reed certainly did everything he could to stoke the fire.

Calvin, in the comic strip *Calvin and Hobbes*, once said:

"The secret of success is being at the right place at the right time. But

since you never know when the right time *is going to be, I figure the trick is to find the right* place, *and just hang around!"*

Maybe I wasn't finding success in my relationships because I was hanging around in all the wrong places. Did I really want to be gay? Did I really want to spend the rest of my life with a man? Or would I rather have a life-long relationship with a woman?

What felt like ultimate freedom at first was beginning to feel like ultimate bondage. I started feeling trapped in a lifestyle I wasn't sure I wanted to live anymore. Even if I *did* want out now, did I still have that choice? And how could I find out?

Chapter 5:

Skinny Dipping

After this series of homosexual relationships, I asked one of my gay friends what he thought about the possibility of leaving homosexuality and having a life-long relationship with a woman. He told me, unequivocally: "Once gay, always gay, Nick." The best thing I could do, he said, was to accept this fact: if I had sex with a man, then I was definitely gay. There was nothing I could do to change it. My friend said that everyone he knew who had ever gone into homosexuality had never come out of it—and the sooner I accepted that fact, the better off I'd be.

I wasn't so sure. I still thought it would be great to get married to a woman and someday have a family with her. I had already kissed several women and loved it. I had just never had sex with them. It seemed to me that sex would be just as fun with a woman. I was just hesitant to try. I didn't want kids anytime soon, and sexual intercourse with a woman could lead to that quickly no matter what kind of protection we used. I also cared about women's hearts, probably more so than men's. I didn't want women to think I was only interested in them for sex, like so many of my friends had complained about.

But now I began to wonder if there was a way to test this out—to find out if I would always be gay or if I could have sex with a women and enjoy that, too. Although I came close to having some encounters like that before, I never felt strong enough about any of the women that I dated to cross the line into sexual exploration.

There was one woman, however, who had, at one point,

expressed an interest in having a casual sexual relationship with me. No commitment required. I didn't take her up on it before, but I liked her enough, so I thought I'd give her a call.

I had met Kelly during a summer musical we were doing at a nearby town. After practice one night, we went to a party at a friend's private pond. Kelly was a few years older than me, and when my friend suggested having a party at his pond, Kelly said, "Yeah, let's go have some fun! Let's not think about anything; let's just have some fun." Sounded great to me! I had no idea her idea of "having some fun" involved sexual intimacy, at least not until we got to the pond and some of the guys suggested we all go skinny dipping.

My friends took off their clothes and dove into the water, so Kelly and I joined them. I could never quite figure out before that night why so many guys were attracted to her. She was always warm and friendly with me and others, but for some reason, she was *really* popular. That night, I discovered her secret! At one point, as I was sitting on the dock, watching my friends jump and splash and swim in the water, Kelly came up and sat down next to me. She pulled the towel off one of my shoulders and put it around her and me both. We were totally naked, other than that towel. I had never sat next to a naked woman before—and certainly not while I was naked, too!

I was petrified and exhilarated at the same time. I tried not to look at her, but just let her talk. When I did glance at her, I couldn't help but glimpse her soft, round breasts so beautifully highlighted by the moon. Everything in me wanted to reach out and touch her and pull her even closer, but I just sat there, stock still. My other friends were still swimming around, so it was just the two of us, sitting and talking and laughing (with my laughs being a little higher and more nervous than hers, it seemed). But when I didn't take her up on any of her obvious queues for "fun without thinking," we got back in the water and swam some more; then the night was over.

But I thought of that night many, many times afterwards, usually kicking myself for not reaching out and touching her breasts and the rest of her totally naked body when her invitation was so clear. *What would it have been like,* I often wondered? *Why didn't I do it when I had the chance?* That night she had become so suddenly beautiful and alluring in my mind—and in reality.

Now here I was, several years later, well on my way down the road of homosexuality. The words of my gay friend kept ringing in my ears: "Once gay, always gay, Nick." Yet I couldn't help thinking that it didn't have to be this way. My mind kept coming back to that night with Kelly, sitting on the dock in the moonlight and with nothing but a towel wrapped around us. She seemed so eager and willing to do whatever I wanted—and all I did was jump back into the pond!

So I called her up. I asked her if I could come visit, that I had some questions about life and sex and wondered if she could help me out. She said she'd love to see me, so we set up a date to meet a few weeks later. When that day came, I drove to another state to get to her apartment, then began to lay out for her everything that had happened to me over the previous few years. I told her that I had entered into several homosexual relationships, and that I wasn't sure if that's what I really wanted out of life. Did she think that what my gay friend said was true, that once I went into homosexuality, I could never come out? Especially in light of the fact that I had felt such excitement when I was sitting next to her naked body several years before? And if she thought I *could* come out of it, would she be willing to help me? I thought that if I had sex with her and absolutely loved it, then it would prove to me, and to my friends, that there *was* another way, that I didn't have to be gay forever if I didn't want to be.

She was gracious and polite and thought it was "cute" that I had come to visit. But she didn't think that I had anything to worry about at all. She was dating another man at the time, and said that it wouldn't be right for her to do anything sexual with me—even though she said she thought the cause was certainly worthy! We settled instead for a glass of wine and some strawberries dipped in chocolate. Before I left, however, she did give me a long, passionate kiss that was as convincing as anything else to that point in my life that I didn't have to feel bound to homosexuality!

I drove home that night with hope in my heart that there just might be another path for me. Although I was disappointed I didn't get a chance to fully "prove" it to myself, I was encouraged that I probably could do it if I wanted to. Perhaps I *did* have a choice after all. I went back to the U of I that semester looking forward to whatever might be in store for me next. But the fiery debate in my mind about what the future held was about to heat up a few more degrees.

I had moved out of the fraternity at the end of the previous summer, deciding instead to move into an apartment with another guy in my pledge class. He and I had seen enough disturbing things at the house that summer that neither of us were convinced that frat life was for us.

Instead, I decided to join a co-ed professional business fraternity that met each week as part of our business school. They didn't have a house where you could live, but simply met for business meetings and social activities. I was able to meet a whole new group of people there, getting to know several of them better as we began our spring semester.

One guy in particular seemed to stand out from the rest. Tim was confident, bold and business minded, but he also seemed a bit too gay in the way he dressed and talked and carried himself. And if he was gay, it was the kind of homosexuality that rubbed me the wrong way, in part because I wanted him to "man-up" a bit, and in part, perhaps, because I was afraid that if I hung out with him too much, people might think I was gay, too—which I was hoping to avoid if I could. I was still pretty quiet about my homosexual feelings and very selective with whom I shared them.

In the months that followed, a group of us always seemed to end up going out together and I found myself spending more and more time with Tim. We got closer and closer in our friendship, and soon we were talking openly about all of our thoughts about homosexuality, too. It felt good to be able to find someone with whom I could be totally comfortable and who would accept me and my gifts and my talents, admiring me for who I was rather than belittling me for who I wasn't. He even loved theater and music and had just finished producing one of the musicals on campus.

Then one day it happened. Tim and I crossed the line from being just friends to being intimate as well. As much as I wanted to resist him—for the sake of how it might look to others—being with him met such a deep need within me that I didn't care so much what others might think about it, or so I thought. We never told anyone that our friendship had taken a sexual turn, and we were keeping our various rendezvous as hidden as possible.

When a mutual friend asked me if I was more than just friends with Tim, I felt like she was accusing me of being something akin to an axe murderer. I didn't know how she'd react if I told her the truth, and I didn't know if she'd be able to understand that we really did love and care for each other. So rather than have her think of me as some kind of criminal, I lied. I didn't want to be found out, and even though she said it really didn't matter to her—that she had just heard a rumor and wondered if it was true—I felt like it really *did* matter to her more than she was letting on.

Shortly thereafter, I got a call from another friend—this one from high school—saying that she had heard I was gay, too. Again, I denied it. "I'm not gay," I said, perhaps a little too categorically. I was saying it in part to my friend and in part to myself, thinking that I hadn't fully committed to that lifestyle yet. And I *did* still have feelings for women, didn't I, even if I hadn't taken the chance to act on them?

Was I gay or was I not? The question was starting to tear me apart, and I felt like I had to make a decision soon. I didn't *want* to stay on the path of homosexuality, but it did feel like it was meeting a valid need in my life for close, male friends. It was fun, too, I had to admit that. But was it something I wanted for the rest of my life?

And what about all those feelings I had when I *did* take the chance to kiss other women—especially those feelings I felt so strongly that night I went skinny dipping with Kelly? Weren't those feelings just as real and just as strong as my homosexual ones, even if I had never acted on them? I could feel myself getting torn apart as I tried to reconcile these two irreconcilable desires within me.

My world was about to change for the good, however, when I invited yet another friend from that same business fraternity to take a road trip with me that summer to the East Coast.

Her name was Noël.

PART 2 ~ CLIMBING OUT

Chapter 6:

Water's Edge

I met Noël a year before we took our fortuitous road trip to the East Coast. We were both attending our first meeting of the professional business fraternity we had joined, a meeting which was being held in a classroom on the second floor of Commerce West (Room 245, to be exact), one of the buildings where we took business classes during the day. Noël was a sophomore and I was a junior, both in the College of Business at the U of I.

My roommate asked me to keep an eye out for Noël at the meeting. He knew her from their weekly get-togethers at Double Dipski's, a local ice cream shop where Noël and her sister met with my roommate and his brother for brownie-unders (a chocolate brownie under a scoop of vanilla ice cream, topped with whipped cream and chocolate sauce). My roommate knew both Noël and I were new to the fraternity, so he thought we should find each other at the meeting.

That wasn't hard for me to do. We were all asked to introduce ourselves by combining the name of a fruit with our own names. Noël introduced herself as "Navel (Orange) Noël" and I introduced myself as "Nectarine Nick." (So much for the "professional" part of our "professional business fraternity"! But it did help us to remember each other's names.)

We found each other at the end of the meeting, but hardly had time to say "Hi" and then it was time to go. I thought Noël was cute and friendly, with a pretty smile and a bouncy perm in her light brown hair. But Noël went home that night, called one of her best friends and told her she had just met the man she was going to marry. Why? Because she said the moment she met me she heard a voice in her head saying, "That's the man you're going to marry." She was so surprised to hear the voice that she wondered who was talking to her!

"If I had thought that myself," she told her friend, "I would have said, 'That's the man *I'm* going to marry.' But the voice clearly said, 'That's the man *you're* going to marry.'" It *had* to be God, she told her friend. And if so, it was the clearest word she had ever heard from God in her life.

It took me a little longer to get the message (I'm sure I wasn't listening), but I did love hanging out with Noël. One of our first outings together was to see a hypnotist at the Illini Union Building. The hypnotist convinced a small group from the audience that they had lost their belly buttons. The people were so distraught about losing their belly buttons that they ran all over the room trying to find them! Noël and I laughed so hard that night.

We went out a few other times, for brownie-unders at Double Dipski's or to basketball games at the Assembly Hall. One night, after spending a whole day with Noël at a business fraternity event, I walked her home to her apartment and gave her a goodnight kiss at the door. But I didn't think much would come of it.

It wasn't until the following summer, when Noël and I went horseback riding one sunny afternoon at a riding stable near the school, that I told her about my plans to visit my sister on the East Coast the next month. I knew Noël loved to travel, so I asked her if she wanted to come along. "Sure!" she said.

So the next month we started off on our ten-hour trip out east. When we got to my sister's house, my sister started asking me all about Noël, assuming we were romantically involved. "Oh, no!" I told her, "we're just friends." Noël was fun and all, but I wasn't interested in her in a romantic or sexual way. (I didn't tell my sister that I was actually dating someone else at that time—and that his name was Tim).

Noël and I had a great time touring the city, going white-water rafting and seeing some concerts at an outdoor theater on a hillside near my sister's home. (One night we saw Frankie Valli, an old-timer to us, singing "Can't Take My Eyes Off of You." Another night we saw Peabo Bryson singing his then-current hit with Roberta Flack "Tonight, I Celebrate My Love for You." It was all so romantic—even though we weren't!)

After spending a few days with my sister, Noël and I drove a couple more hours to spend a few days at Myrtle Beach.

When we got to the beach, we tried to check into a hotel, but the clerk said we couldn't share a room because we weren't married. "We're just friends!" I protested. But the clerk said it was hotel policy, and she was sorry. We couldn't get a room together. Noël and I had packed a tent in our trunk for the trip, so I asked if there were any campgrounds nearby. She told us about a state park a few miles away, also near the beach, so we set out again, found the campground and pitched our tent. Then we headed for the beach.

It was too late to swim, but the sun hadn't gone down yet, so we took off for a stroll along the water's edge. Noël and I walked for miles along the beach, talking and laughing and sharing our dreams and visions for our lives as we watched the sun set. When the conversation turned to love, Noël asked if there was anyone special in my life. I couldn't tell her I was dating Tim! So I talked about another woman I had met at school (and with whom I had become pretty infatuated, actually). I went on and on, talking way too much about this woman's incredible qualities, not realizing that Noël was on the vacation of her dreams with the man she felt God had told her she was going to marry!

But by the time we got back to the spot where we had started our walk, something had changed. I had brought a bottle of wine on the trip, so we got it out of the car and sat down on the beach. Whether it was the wine and the waves, the moon and the stars, or just Noël's delicious-looking lips, I kissed her. And she returned my kiss. It was luscious.

I don't know how long we kissed like that, but I do know what happened next. Noël reached over, and without saying a word, she set her hand on my lap—directly in the center! In the past, I would have been petrified, frozen, by something like this. But not that night. All I felt was utter delight. That night went on to become one of the most romantic and memorable nights of my entire life.

I couldn't believe this was Noël, sweet Noël, with her bouncy, little-girl curls in her hair. As we sat there on the beach, she looked like she could have been playing a game in a great big sandbox. But that kiss—that touch! There was nothing "little-girl" about her. My view of Noël, the world and my future all changed simultaneously that night. And the next night. And the next.

Although we never made love in the fullest sense on that trip, we certainly enjoyed ourselves without reserve, right up to and including the point where we were both fully satisfied in our unexpected, newfound love. As we drove back to Illinois, we listened—over and over—to a cassette tape Noël had brought with her. The tape was of an R&B group she loved called Midnight Star. The tagline to one of their songs was "Let me hear you say, 'Oh!'" We sang it over and over, and all I could think of on that trip back home was "Oh, Noël O!" (as her last name began with O.) We went to the coast as just friends, but came home as something much, much more. I had never experienced anything as satisfying or joy-filled in my life.

When we got back to Illinois, I was now faced with the dilemma of my life. Homosexuality was meeting some deep, deep needs for close friendships with other guys, and I didn't want to give that up. But something about my time with Noël was meeting a need that seemed even deeper still—and I didn't want to turn back on that, either. So I did what many other teenagers do when their hormones are raging and they can't decide whether to date one person or another: I dated both.

Tim was glad to see me when I got home, but he asked me, point blank, if I had slept with Noël while I was gone. I couldn't deny it. I told him I did. Tim was hurt and asked what I was going to do. I told him I didn't know, but that I didn't want to lose him. He was my best friend at the time. And Tim didn't want to lose me, so for the first few months of that fall semester, I dated them both. Noël had no idea, of course, and Tim was doing what he could to make the most of it.

For a while I felt like I had the best of both worlds. One night I would go to Noël's apartment and be intimate with her. The next night I would sneak away and be intimate with Tim.

But something within me knew this was wrong. Even if I accepted the idea that homosexuality was okay, I wasn't okay with dating two people at the same time—especially when one of them had no idea about my secret, homosexual life. It just didn't seem right.

The struggle in my brain grew stronger and stronger and was about to peak. Our business fraternity was sponsoring a barn dance that fall, and all three of us were planning to attend. I was taking Noël as my date, but I was also planning a secret outing with Tim afterward.

It was too much for my little brain to take. I knew I had to make a decision. But what should I do? Was I going to pursue Noël and a possible life of heterosexuality? Or was I going to keep going out with Tim and possibly stay in homosexuality forever?

It was time to decide. And I had no idea what I was going to do.

Chapter 7:
Tension Mounts

The weeks leading up to the barn dance were some of the most intense weeks of my life. I was getting closer than ever to *both* Tim and Noël, emotionally and physically. I loved my relationship with each of them, and I didn't want to have to decide between them. At the same time, I knew this was bigger than just deciding between Tim and Noël. This decision had the potential to determine the course of the rest of my life—and I knew it.

I wished so badly that I could talk to someone about it, but I didn't know who could help. The only people who knew about my homosexual attractions were my gay friends, and they had already voiced their opinions ("Once gay, always gay"). I thought about talking to one of the pastors at a church on campus, but I couldn't bring myself to do it. I had no idea what they would really think about it anyway, as I had never heard a pastor preach about it—whether for it *or* against it—and I had never read what the Bible had to say about it.

I had a great relationship with my mom and dad, and I usually talked to them about everything in my life, but this was different. I couldn't imagine talking to them about my sex life, let alone my *homosexual* sex life. We had never talked about homosexuality, and it was hardly discussed much of anywhere at that time. The first time I heard the word homosexual on TV, I had to look it up in the dictionary to find out that it described someone who had feelings of sexual attraction for a person of the same sex. Although that's how I felt towards men, I also had attractions towards women, especially now towards Noël. I didn't want to worry my parents by telling them about my attractions to men, but I didn't want to tell them I was sleeping with Noël, either!

And although I had straight friends I could have talked to, most of them knew Tim, and he would have been devastated if they found out about our relationship.

So I was stuck. My heart was burning to talk to someone (anyone!) about it, but I felt like I had no one. The best I could do was to try to figure it out for myself.

For starters, I wanted to separate the personalities of the people I was dating from the bigger question of homosexuality versus heterosexuality. I didn't want to make a lifetime decision based on the particular pros or cons of Tim versus Noël, because I felt the real question was so much bigger. The real question was, "Did I want to pursue a lifetime of homosexuality or a lifetime of heterosexuality?"

On the "pro" side for homosexuality, it did help me to meet a legitimate need I had for close male friends, a need that was met to overflowing by some of the gay friends I knew up to this point. It felt so good to be loved and affirmed for my creative gifts, and to be understood by guys who also felt alienated from the men that surrounded them. And the sex part was great, too! I was happy to be gay in the happiest sense of the word. I had also never engaged in anal intercourse with a man or in anything else that made sex with men feel dirty, painful or in any way that made me feel demeaned or "feminized" by what we were doing. My sexual interaction with men would be best described as "mutual masturbation." And for me, since masturbation felt good, then doing it with a close friend felt even better. I referred to some of my friends at that time as "kissable friends" (or as others called it, "friends with benefits"). If I was going to be friends with someone, wasn't it natural to take it to the next level and please each other in physical ways, too? *What's wrong with that?* I thought.

My view was reinforced when I went to see Madeline

Murray O'Hair speak on campus one night, the woman who had won a Supreme Court victory to take prayer out of public school. She was a powerhouse of a speaker and her mantra throughout the night was simply, "If it feels good, do it!" (Unfortunately for her, a few years later one of her employees took her mantra to heart, venting all his frustrations out on her, and hacking her to death into tiny pieces which he then buried on a Texas ranch. As sad as that was—for no one should have to experience such a gruesome death—Ms. O'Hair's employee was just following her own advice: apparently it felt good to him, so he did it.) But the night I heard her speak, it all made perfect sense to me, and to most of the cheering crowd of college students listening with me who were happy to have someone affirm their promiscuity. *If I want to have sex with my friends,* I thought, *whether they're men or women, what's wrong with that?* I loved the adventure of it all, even the heightened intrigue I felt by my secret, homosexual encounters.

On the "con" side of homosexuality, however, that same secrecy was one of its biggest drawbacks. When I brought my college friends home to visit my parents on the farm, I was never able to tell them, "This is my good friend so and so, and by the way, he's a *really* good friend of mine. I *really* like him, and I wanted you to meet him." It just never seemed appropriate to share how significant these men were to me in my life, and not being able to share about the depth of our friendships was disappointing.

I didn't know if I could go through a lifetime of being in a secret homosexual relationship, and I couldn't imagine being open about it with my family and friends. None of the guys I had dated so far were open about their homosexual attractions, and the thought of being open about it was simply unthinkable to me. Could I live this life of secrecy all my life, not letting even my family and best friends know about someone who was so special to me?

At the same time, I liked the idea of having kids and a family of my own someday. Even though I wasn't ready for kids at that point, I did love being part of a family growing up. I loved my parents, I loved my brother and sister and I loved doing all the things that we did together as a family, from playing games and doing chores to opening Christmas presents and taking family vacations. I loved being part of a family and I imagined having a family of my own someday.

A life of homosexuality, however, seemed to automatically preclude that option. I didn't personally know of *any* gay people who had kids. Every gay relationship I saw was a dead-end street in that regard. All I saw for a future on that path was two men living together forever, if it lasted that long, and then came the end. While homosexuality offered some genuine benefits to me in the short run, I felt like I would be missing out on a whole lot of major life experiences in the long run.

Heterosexuality, on the other hand, offered me the two things I really wanted for my future: 1) to be open and honest to others about my relationship with another person who meant the most to me in the world, and 2) to be able to fulfill the idea of having kids and a family of my own. Both of these were huge benefits of heterosexuality to me; and while they were still a ways off in the future, they helped me see which path I'd rather be on—especially now that it was fully apparent to me that I *had* that choice. As far as sexual excitement goes, Noël had shown me that heterosexuality offered me just as much passion and pleasure, if not more so, starting with that off-the-charts night at Myrtle Beach and the many months that followed.

In the short term, both paths seemed about equally attractive. But in the long term, heterosexuality won out, while homosexuality looked like a dead end. If all other things were equal, and I could really pick between either path, which would I pick? Having laid out both paths as fully as I could in my mind, the scales tipped heavily in favor of heterosexuality.

But before I made a final decision, I wanted to figure out the answer to one more question: If I *did* pick the path of heterosexuality, was Noël the one whom I should pursue on that path? Could I imagine spending the rest of my life *with her*?

Even though I wasn't ready for marriage yet, I felt that if I *was* going to start walking down this path, I wanted to make sure it was with someone with whom I could see the *potential* of staying with forever.

Noël, I had found, was more than just delightful. She was a *riot*. She was funny, she was fun and she was super cute. More than that, she loved me—*adored* me, really—and not in some kind of fawning, desperate way, but in a way that made me feel truly loved, appreciated, cherished and respected.

As for our physical attraction for each other, whenever we got together, it was nearly impossible to pull us apart. I was still astounded by how much had changed since our trip out east. Before that trip, I thought Noël was pretty, but somewhat plain. After that trip, I couldn't believe I ever thought anything about her was plain! (Tim described her as being "as plain as a piece of Melba Toast." This, however, was coming from a man who wore so much cologne that his father said that when he walked into Tim's room, he thought he was walking into a whorehouse.)

But after our trip together, there was nothing plain about Noël anymore. There was no amount of makeup or jewelry or clothing that could add anything more to her sheer natural beauty. She was gorgeous to me in every sense of the word, both inside and out.

To top it all off, Noël was *smart!* She could read twice as fast as me (when we would try to read a book together, she would finish both pages before I got to the bottom of the first page). And she could do math in her head four times faster than me (she always knew if a clerk had applied a coupon or not to a shopping cart full of groceries because she knew the total of everything in her cart before we got to the checkout lane).

Studying came harder to her than to me, however, and I would frequently try to talk her out of going to our COBOL 310 programming classes so we could go for a walk on the quad instead, or take a picnic lunch to Busey Woods, where we would share a couple of wine coolers and more than a few kisses.

For Noël, our time together was a chance for her to break out of the routine of college life. At first, I thought she was a bit of a loner, spending most of her time studying or going for an occasional brownie-under with her sister and my roommate. But after I got to know her better, I found out that in high school she was involved in nearly every kind of activity she could possibly do, whether cheerleading or dance or various scholastic clubs. Noël was so popular, in fact, that her high school class of 400+ students elected her to be their prom queen in her senior year. All this from a girl who, when I first met her, appeared to be so quiet and unassuming. I felt like I might have discovered a hidden jewel in Noël, a rare princess in disguise.

I was ready and willing to find out. After thinking it through as best as I possibly could, I made my decision. Now came the part that was even harder: telling both Tim and Noël what was on my heart. Tim was my best friend, and I knew this would break his heart. And as much as I loved Noël and wanted to tell her of my heartfelt commitment to her, I also felt that if I were to pursue this any further, I would have to confess to her that I had been seeing someone else the whole time that I had been seeing her—and that the someone else was our mutual friend Tim.

I had never faced two more difficult conversations in my life.

Chapter 8:
Feminine Love

I decided to talk to Tim first. The hardest part for me was that he *was* my best friend at the time. The hardest part for him was that there was nothing he could do to change the situation. I tried to assure him that my decision wasn't about him; it was about the kind of life I pictured myself living down the road. Still it hurt him terribly.

Tim had seen this conversation coming and had already braced himself for it. He knew I was moving closer and closer to making a decision between him and Noël, so he wasn't surprised when I finally did.

But no matter what I said, the bottom line was that this was not only the end of our dating relationship, but most likely the end of our friendship, too. I couldn't imagine trying to maintain a purely platonic relationship with him if I was going to truly pursue Noël. Tim and I had gone too far to try to just back up a little.

When I left his apartment that night, I said goodbye not only to Tim, but also to a way of life that I knew would never get me where I wanted to go. Even though I still loved some things about homosexuality, I felt like this was the right next step for me towards what I really wanted in life.

In many ways I was "betting the farm" on my relationship with Noël—which made the prospect of an already difficult conversation with her all the more difficult. What if I blew it?

When I got together the next night with Noël, I was more nervous than ever. I told her there was something I wanted to talk to her about, but when the time came to do it, I didn't know if I could. But if I was going to try to live an authentic life with her, I wanted to be completely honest with her about this, too. After sitting fairly dumbstruck with her on the couch for a while, talking about everything other than what I needed to talk to her about, I finally asked her if we could go for a walk. I knew I was making it worse by delaying it any longer, and she was starting to wonder what I could possibly have to tell her that was so difficult. Was I going to break up with her? Had I done something horrific that she would want to break up with me? She tried to fill in the gaps in her mind, which made a hard situation even worse.

When I finally told her about my homosexual attractions and that I had slept with several men over the past few years— including the fact that I was dating Tim the whole time I was dating her—up until I broke things off with him the night before—her response astounded me.

She was surprised and she was hurt, but mostly she was hurting for me. She saw the pain of my struggle and she wanted to make it all better.

I told her she already had, and that I wanted so much to pursue a life of heterosexuality—and I wanted to pursue it with her—if she was willing to pursue it with me. She was! She loved me, she said, and she wanted nothing more than to be with me, no matter what I was going through.

Of all the responses I could have gotten, that was the most unexpected. Of course she felt hurt by my dating both her and Tim, but the homosexuality didn't seem to bother her nearly as much as it bothered me, if it bothered her at all. She just loved me, and she was so glad that I wanted to keep pursuing my relationship with her.

Rather than pushing me away as I had feared, Noël drew me closer and closer with her response. That conversation also launched us into a whole new level of intimacy. I was no longer holding anything back from her. Noël knew everything about me, and she loved me still! I was amazed, relieved and overwhelmed all at once.

I thought I loved Noël before that night, but my love for her—and my respect—went higher and higher.

In the months that followed, my new relationship with Noël brought three things into my life that I hadn't anticipated. First, it felt so good to be able to be open and honest with other people about the person I was dating. After a string of six, secretive, homosexual relationships of varying lengths over the previous two years, I was finally able to tell others about the person who was most precious to me in the world. When our friends saw us happy together, it made them happy, too. In comparison, this felt so much better. This felt good. This felt right. It felt like I was "coming home"—home to the way things were supposed to be.

Second, I discovered a new level of love that I hadn't known before. When I would get close to a man who understood me and accepted me and loved me, that was something special. But this was something different. This was love on another plane—love with potential, love with a future, love that was going somewhere and could grow someday to become even wider and taller as we considered adding a family to it. It was a kind of love that was boundless on various measures.

Third, and most thrilling of all, I found Noël's femininity to be totally adorable. She was soft and smooth and oh-so-feminine in all the right places. She was sweet to kiss, beautiful to look at and totally fun to be with. Although neither of us had ever had full sexual intercourse with each other or with anyone else, we did explore each other's bodies as fully as possible otherwise, with all of the subtle (and not-so-subtle) responses that such exploration produced. I never appreciated the interconnections that are hard-wired into a woman's body, and how touching one part of her body would excite her in another part. It was all so fascinating and new to me, this

feminine love, which I was discovering for the first time.
Even though Noël and I both had roommates at school, we
found no shortage of places and ways to be alone and be
intimate, whether at one of our apartments or on a blanket in
the woods or on a late-night date on the quad in a secluded
spot (I worked on the grounds crew, so I knew where those
secluded spots were!). During all our times that we were able to
enjoy each other so passionately, there were only two things I
wished were different: 1) I wished I could go "all the way" with
her (neither of us felt we should) and 2) I wished I never had
to say goodnight.

I couldn't get enough of her, and she couldn't get enough
of me. We were madly, ecstatically and passionately in love on
every level: relationally, emotionally and—without a doubt—
physically.

I wrote a poem to Noël one day using a computer at the
political science office where I worked part time. The
computer was an Apple Lisa, the predecessor to the Apple
Macintosh, which had just been introduced in their famous
Superbowl commercial earlier that year. The Apple Lisa was
the first computer I had ever used on which I could type and
draw pictures in the same document. I wrote and illustrated my
first poem to Noël:

I love your name Noël
You don't look like a Navel (and I drew a picture of an orange).
Your hair is so curly,
You never look squirrel-y (and I drew a picture of a squirrel).
I'm thankful for much and all that life teaches,
But mostly for you, white wine and beaches (and I drew a picture of
the two of us walking and holding hands).

While it may have sounded sophomoric (I was a senior at
the time!), Noël held onto that poem, and loved re-reading it
from time to time, for it captured our time together on the
coast when we first fell in love.

As the spring semester approached, and with it my upcoming graduation from the U of I, I had no idea what the future held.

All I knew was that I wanted to hold onto Noël.

Chapter 9:
Bubble Gum

By the time I graduated, I had two job offers: one in Houston, Texas (1,000 miles away) working in the computer department of a large, international oil company; and the other in Dhaka, Bangladesh (8,000 miles away) working as a computer consultant for a disease research center. Either way, I was going to have to leave Noël behind, as she still had one more year of college to finish. It was going to be the hardest thing to do. I loved her so much, and I didn't want to be away from her for even a day.

Noël was heading overseas that fall, too, however, as she had applied for and been accepted to the same school in Salzburg, Austria, where I had studied two years earlier. The job at the research center in Bangladesh was only for three months, with a possible extension of several more months, if necessary. And the oil company in Houston said their offer was a standing offer, so I could go to work for them whenever I was done with my consulting job in Bangladesh. So I decided to do both.

The week before I graduated, I got a telegram from the research center in Bangladesh asking if I could come the next week. So three days after graduation, without skipping a beat, I was catapulted out of college and into a whole new world.

Everything about that trip to Bangladesh was amazing, from riding rickshaws through the crowded streets (dodging people, goats and speeding cars), to house-sitting for international families (in their British-style homes in an Indian-style country). I had to get used to the idea of having up to four servants at times: a cook, a bearer (who served the food), a chowkidar (who was a watchman who opened the gate) and a mali (who was a gardener who cut the grass around the house —using either a pair of scissors or a pair of goats, depending on the day). It didn't take me long to get used to it, though, as I could hardly have lived there without them—and some of them became great friends.

I showed pictures of Noël to my bearer one day and asked if he was in love with anyone, too. He said he wasn't, that it was too much responsibility at that time, but that his father was looking for a wife for him. One woman loved him, but her education level was too low. Another loved him, but she wasn't pretty. He told me I should be thankful for such a beautiful woman who was at the same educational level as I was. Hearing his perspective made me love Noël all the more.

My days were filled with work and my nights and weekends with explorations of the new, eye-opening world around me. I took morning walks with two of the center's directors through the slums around the research center. They told me all about the culture, the people and the work they were doing. I had never seen such poverty in my life, juxtaposed with so many smiles from nearly everyone we met. In talking with my bearer about the difficult conditions in his country, I said that I knew of many people in America with more money, but who did not smile so much. He said, in broken English:

"Money does not happy make—that is universal truth."

My office was in the "animal house" of the center, the place where they kept the animals that were used for research. We had computers at one end of the building and bleating goats, squawking chickens and chattering monkeys at the other end. Silicon Valley this wasn't! It was more like a cattle barn back home at the 4-H fair, complete with all the sounds and smells that went along with it.

I loved taking it all in, from trying new foods like lichee and jack fruit and having a bowlful of mangoes and pineapple cut up every morning by my cook, to exploring the markets and buying spices sold by the scoopful and meat hanging from hooks. (I was extra thankful when I first went to the market that my cook did the shopping, too.)

But as the weeks turned to months, the newness began to wear off, and I started to see how truly difficult it was for the people who lived there, especially for my Bengali friends who worked at the center and were restricted by their government from leaving. They felt hopelessly stuck in a country where fresh water was scarce and open sewers that poured into the streets were prolific. I grew more and more thankful for my life back home in the States, missing Noël all the more. We wrote letters back and forth and called each other when we could. (I had to ask an operator to place a call to the States, and they would call me back, sometimes ten or fifteen minutes later when they found an open line.) I loved hearing Noël's voice. We would laugh and shout into the phone, trying to be heard and trying to see who could say "I love you" the most times in a single conversation.

When my three months in Bangladesh were almost over, my contract was renewed for another two months, so Noël and I resigned ourselves to not seeing each other for a while longer. Noël was leaving for Salzburg soon (as I had somehow inspired her to go there, too). So I wouldn't get to see her till we were both back in Illinois at Christmas. I told her I could try to visit Salzburg on my way home, but then I had a better idea! Why didn't she come to Bangladesh for a week on her fall break, then we'd travel back together to Salzburg for a few days on my way home to the States? She loved the idea, so we began making plans.

The idea of Noël coming to Bangladesh also helped me to begin seeing the country through her eyes, knowing that she'd soon be there with me, which made it much more bearable.

In the time between my two consulting contracts, I decided to take a week off with a few of the other international workers at the center to travel to the neighboring country of India. We all wanted to see what India was like, so we booked a flight to Calcutta and then a train ride to the hill station of Darjeeling where they grew and picked the world-famous Darjeeling tea.

When we landed in Calcutta—which is sometimes described as one of the dirtiest cities in the world—it seemed clean in comparison to Dhaka, where I had just been, making the poverty of Bangladesh seem all the more desperate. Then taking the train up to the hill country of Darjeeling was like taking a ride up to heaven. The view was spectacular and the people were beautiful with their small stature, dark eyes and smooth, dark skin stretched taut over their faces.

We stayed at a beautiful lodge in the foothills of the Himalayas, with fireplaces in the bedrooms and hot water bottles delivered nightly and placed under our warm woolen comforters. We drank the aromatic Darjeeling tea for breakfast, then ventured out for the highlight of our trip: an eight-hour horseback ride to Tiger Hill through the Himalayan mountains and fields of tea. I loved it so much that I took another ten-hour horseback ride the following day to the neighboring state of Sikkim.

I had never done anything like that before, galloping on narrow paths through the clouds at 7,100 feet on some of the steepest mountains I had ever seen. Galloping around one of the curves, I saw the most breathtaking sight of all: tall waterfalls up ahead and tiny villages down below, with the mist from the clouds hanging all around. I felt like I was riding through a picture in a *National Geographic* magazine. "Spectacular" is a good word to start describing what my friends and I were seeing, but my friends and I started making up words to try to describe it, as there weren't enough superlatives in English to come close to capturing the sight. Laurie Anderson, a contemporary, avant-garde musician at the time, said she often felt like a piece of bubble gum being stretched: the tension kept pulling her back, but the adventure was in seeing how far she could stretch.

I felt exactly the same. I loved the adventure of seeing how far I could stretch, yet the tension kept pulling me back to the things I loved: my home, my life in America and especially Noël. When I got back to Bangladesh, Noël and I could hardly wait to see each other again.

The month before she came, I remembered what a friend's mother had told me whenever she was separated from those she loved:

"It never seems bad to be away from people when you won't see them for a long time. But when the time gets close to seeing them again, and you can almost touch it, that's when you go crazy waiting."

I was one month away from seeing Noël again. And I was going crazy waiting.

Chapter 10:
Burning Flames

Noël and I practically burst into flames with pent-up passion when she stepped off the plane in Bangladesh. We spent the first week touring around the city, riding in rickshaws, eating rice and dal with our hands and coming home every night to enjoy each other in every way. I couldn't stop looking at her and touching her. She was so beautiful.

Noël didn't believe me when I told her she didn't need to bring any shorts to wear on the trip. Even though the temperatures could easily reach 100 degrees Fahrenheit, none of the women in Bangladesh wore shorts. Noël packed a few pairs of shorts anyway, telling me that she figured she'd just try to blend in with the other tourists. The trouble was, there were no other tourists!

Noël and I thought it was ironic that the official travel posters for the country tried to turn their greatest problem (no tourists) into something positive by posting pictures of palm trees and beaches, saying, "Come to Bangladesh before the tourists do." (Another poster we saw described one of the local hotels as "Dhaka's *first* luxury hotel." The poster down the street for the same hotel was perhaps a little more honest, calling it, "Dhaka's *only* luxury hotel.")

But having Noël there with me made Bangladesh one of the hottest destination spots in the world. We ate our dinners together, cooked by my cook and served by my bearer. We watched sunsets together while sitting on the flat roof of my house. And we took showers together, using water heated by the sun in storage tanks on the rooftop during the day. If I didn't have enough English words to describe the views in

Darjeeling, I for sure didn't have words to describe the views I was now seeing back in Bangladesh—now that Noël was in them.

It wasn't all fun and games, however, as the poverty all around us was still so desperate. Noël cried one day when she saw a mother holding her baby. The baby looked so thin neither of us could believe it was possibly still alive. We also saw life outside of the city when we went by train several hours away to visit the hometown village of one of my cooks. The villagers were so happy to see us, in part because I had helped my cook and my friend, Robi, to buy two lengths of pipe to add to the three he had already bought so they could put in their first freshwater well for their village. I was able to help them the day they installed the well, so when I came back with Noël, the villagers treated us like royalty. They were so taken with Noël and her milk-white skin, they asked if they could touch her arms, saying they wished their skin was so light. Noël, of course, being so white all her life, said she honestly wished her skin was dark like theirs. Seeing how much the villagers loved Noël boosted my love for her even more, if that were possible.

After several days in Bangladesh, we took a trip to the nearby country of Nepal. I had heard from the director of our center that his favorite trip he had ever taken with his family was to Terai Jungle in Nepal, crashing through the jungle on the backs of elephants. I was sold immediately and wanted to go, too!

So Noël and I took an hour and a half flight from Dhaka to Kathmandu, a Shangri-La type of city in the mountaintops of the Himalayas. On our flight into Kathmandu, we saw a close-up view of Mount Everest, the world's tallest mountain. (When we landed in Kathmandu, we got a close-up look at what had to be one of the world's smallest airports—and shortest runways!)

We spent a day and a night in Kathmandu, visiting Hindu temples and eating at restaurants which advertised that their salad ingredients had been soaked in iodine for thirty minutes (something which made me excited to eat there because I hadn't been able to eat a salad for months because of diseases in the fresh veggies; but to Noël, salad soaked in iodine didn't sound too appetizing!).

All of this was just a precursor to what had to be one of the most thrilling experiences of my life: spending three days with Noël in the Terai Jungle at a place called Chitwan Jungle Lodge. To get there, we had to take a jeep from Kathmandu to a nearby river, down which we rafted for four hours through the foothills of the Himalayas to the plains of southern Nepal. It was thoroughly relaxing to float through those huge, beautiful mountains, watching monkeys jump from tree to tree on either side, with the warm yellow sun and the sky-blue skies overhead.

When we got to the bottom of the mountains, another jeep picked us up and drove us through rivers, through mud and across the barren plains. At one point, we reached a river that was too wide to cross with no bridge in sight. Noël and I got out of the jeep, wondering what we were going to do next, when we saw three huge elephants lumbering across the river to carry us and our luggage back across to the other side. But the elephants didn't stop when we got to the other side. We rode on their backs for another hour until we finally got to the lodge, where the elephants backed up to a ten-foot platform. We walked right off the elephants' backs onto the platform, where we were greeted by the lodge manager. Although he was definitely Nepali, all I could picture as he welcomed us to his lodge was Ricardo Montalbán on *Fantasy Island* saying, "Welcome to my island!"

We then spent three incredible days in the jungle, sleeping in a thatched hut at night and venturing out into the jungle during the days. We crashed through the forests on the backs of the elephants, just as my director had described, taking off at a run whenever we heard a tiger in the distance, trying to catch a glimpse of one. We never did see a tiger (for which I was simultaneously disappointed and thankful), but we did see plenty of rhino and deer and even got to play with the elephants as they bathed in the rivers, wading alongside them as they spouted water on themselves—and on us—with their trunks.

We tried swinging on vines (only to find that they weren't attached as good as they seemed to be in the movies, and we didn't realize until too late that when we pulled them down, ants and various other crawling creatures would rain down on our heads). We ate dinner with the other guests, watched local dancers out by a huge bonfire (as there was no electricity anywhere at the lodge), and we went to bed early, in our hut, enjoying the nighttime sounds of the jungle outside and the intimate touch of each other's skin inside.

After three of the most astounding days of my life, it was time to head home, back to Bangladesh and then back to the States, with a stopover in Austria to be with Noël for a few more days until we parted again until Christmas.

E.B. White, whose essays I was reading that year, wrote an essay that summed up the way I was feeling. The essay was called "Years of Wonder" and said, in part:

"I wanted to test myself—throw myself into any flame that was handy, to see if I could stand the heat."

I felt like I was doing the same. I was living life to the full, throwing myself into any flame, hoping I didn't get burned.

It was getting hotter at every turn. But so far so good! What could possibly go wrong?

PART 3 ~ REACHING UP

Chapter 11:
Broken Heart

There were no direct flights from Bangladesh to Austria, so Noël and I flew to London first, taking advantage of our long layover there to jump on the Tube—the city's railway system—and head downtown. We saw Buckingham Palace (the home of Queen Elizabeth II) and #10 Downing Street (the home of Prime Minister Margaret Thatcher), then ate breakfast at a café across the street from Big Ben (the home of "Ben," the big bell that chimes out the hours of the day). We had lunch on our next flight, then dinner at a pizzeria by a river in Zurich during another layover. We felt quite cosmopolitan by the time we landed in Salzburg that night (although we decided that we could only earn that title if we could remain coherent in every city in which we stopped. After thirty hours of traveling, we were anything but coherent!)

Salzburg was wonderful. We did nothing but eat in cafés and go shopping for the rest of the week. My sister even came over to spend a few days with us. On the weekend, Noël and I decided to take a train to Vienna to see one of my old roommates, who was now studying in Vienna for the year.

In the backseat of the cab on the way to the train station, I jokingly asked Noël if she had slept with anyone else while I was in Bangladesh. She hesitated and looked down, but when she looked back up, she looked me in my eyes and said, "Yes." Her answer sent a wave of shock throughout my body, and I'm sure it came out in the expression on my face.

What?!? She couldn't be serious! But she was.

She told me about a guy who had asked her out to see a concert in Chicago—Bruce Springsteen's *Born in the USA* tour.

Noël wanted to go see it, so she went. They kissed, then things went further. She ended up spending the night with him.

I was speechless. I couldn't believe it. Why would she *do* that? Why didn't she *tell* me before? How could I have just spent two of the most romantic weeks of my life with her, only to find out now? What was she thinking? What was I thinking? Would she ever have told me if I hadn't asked? I felt trapped in the backseat of that taxi cab. It was cold, it was raining, it was dark and I wanted to scream! I wanted to jump out of the cab, I wanted to jump out of my skin—everything was feeling too tight and too claustrophobic.

I asked her more questions. They hadn't had full intercourse, she said, but they had done everything else. It was just that one night, but it was one night too many for me, one night that changed everything, one night that took me from the highest high of my life to the lowest low in a matter of seconds.

Noël was perplexed by my response. "Didn't you say before you left that it was okay if we wanted to see other people while you were gone?"

Did I *really* say that? Did I *really* think that was okay? I think I did actually say it, now that I thought about it, but how could I possibly think that was okay? I never thought she'd do it! I mean, she loved me. She *adored* me. I couldn't imagine she would ever do anything like that to anyone—and certainly not to me! But she was right. I had said it. I had brought it on myself.

As my world started crashing down upon me, I had a realization: Hadn't I done the same thing to her? Hadn't I been sleeping with someone else when I started sleeping with her—and not just for one night, but for many nights over many months before I finally got up enough nerve to tell her about it? And hadn't I had done the same thing to Tim when I went on that road trip to the East Coast with Noël, sleeping with her when I was still dating him? And hadn't I done the same thing to Mathieu when I went to Salzburg the first time and came back to tell him, so excitedly, about my overseas forays into the wide world of homosexuality?

What Noël had done to me by that act was a small taste of what I had done to her and to others. It all felt so different though, now that I was on the receiving end of the news. I had seen the effects that my confessions had on others, and I knew those to whom I had confessed must have been hurt, but I hadn't felt the pain of it myself—not like this. Now I was seeing the flip side of the same coin that I had so casually tossed into the air.

Noël and I got on the train and went to Vienna. We saw my roommate, saw the art museums and saw the beautiful Vienna Woods, with breathtaking views of its mountains and vineyards. But my mind was constantly filled with images of Noël and whatever must have taken place between her and this other guy. She and I were intimate again that weekend, but the pleasure I would have normally felt was overshadowed by the pain in my heart.

We took another train back to Salzburg, and after a few more days together, I had to leave her again as I flew back to the States while she finished out her semester in Austria. Four flights later, I landed in the U.S. where my parents and a friend picked me up at the airport. As glad as I was to see them, my mind kept going back to Noël and her heartbreaking confession.

Something inside me had snapped. Something had broken. I had run into some kind of invisible law of nature, something I couldn't see, yet something that was as real as the law of gravity. As much as I tried to ignore it before, I could no more ignore it than I could ignore gravity. As much as I tried to convince myself that boundaries in intimate relationships didn't exist, I felt like a man trying to convince himself that gravity didn't exist. Whether I believed in gravity or not, I was still subject to its inherent effects. I couldn't just jump off a ten-story building, thinking that gravity didn't exist, and remain unscathed.

Yet that's just what I felt had happened. I had violated some kind of universal law when I started sleeping with other people so casually. Although the effects didn't hit me as suddenly as if I had tried to defy the law of gravity, they had caught up with me now. It was just a matter of time. I had often wondered about, and argued against, the idea that there were any absolutes in life. Everything was relative, I believed. But I had just bumped into an absolute—or more descriptively, I had smacked right into one, like the surface of the water I had smacked into in Crete. It was wrong to take something so precious and intimate as a sexual relationship and let someone else intrude upon it. Doing so violated the very intimacy that was supposed to be created. If sex was just sex, just a physical act without any love or emotion or commitment tied to it, then why did so many people break up when they found out their lover had sex with someone else? Why did so many long-term marriages break up over one, casual, one-night stand? If sex was just physical pleasure and nothing more, none of those breakups would ever occur. There had to be something more to sexual intimacy, something that went beyond anything I could see or feel or touch, some kind of bond that tied Noël and me together deep in our souls. Now that the bond was broken, it broke my heart and tore it in two.

Like Newton's third law of motion—for every action, there is an equal and opposite reaction—the same seemed to hold true here: the deeper the love, the deeper the pain when it all comes apart.

I loved Noël. I must have written "I love you" more than a thousand times in my letters to her from Bangladesh—and she had written the same in her letters to me. How could she do this? I couldn't get it out of my mind. I also couldn't get it out of my mind that I had done the same thing to her and to several others numerous times. I had been wronged, that's true. But I had done wrong as well. I could hardly bear the weight of it all.

In the weeks following my return to the States, I began to lose so much weight and become so lethargic that my parents finally checked me into a hospital. I was there for a week as they ran all kinds of tests to find out what was wrong with me. The tests showed that I had a combination of mono, non-chronic hepatitis and an intestinal virus, all of which could have certainly added to my meltdown. But the main source of my condition, which I knew, but which the doctors and my family didn't, went much deeper: I was suffering from a broken heart.

After that week in the hospital, I spent the rest of my time, from then until Christmas, resting and recovering, trying to pull myself back together as best I could. I couldn't stop thinking about the situation, and I couldn't find a way out of it. I visited one of my gay friends at the U of I who tried to talk me into feeling better but who knew the pain of betrayal himself. He told me of a relationship in which his partner had confessed to him that he had slept with twelve other men while the two of them were dating. What would *that* feel like—the pain that I now felt multiplied by twelve? I knew the law I had run into was universal—and it was being broken universally, in my life and in the lives of my friends.

As much as I wanted to blame Noël, I knew she had just done what I had given her approval to do. I was the one who had said it was okay to date other people. I was the one who talked her into the idea of "kissable friends," saying it was just the next step in a good and close friendship, even if there was no intention of ever having an exclusive commitment to each other to go along with it. But that *wasn't* okay. That *wasn't* normal, that *wasn't* natural, that *wasn't* the way things were supposed to be. I was in pain, and while Noël shared part of the blame, I knew I shared an even bigger part of it, for I had fueled her in this direction.

A sports star once told his friend that he didn't *want* to be a role model for others. His friend replied:

"It's not a matter of whether you want to be a role model or not. You are a role model. The question is whether you're going to be a good role model or a bad one."

I realized I was in the same spot as that sports star. I was a role model all right, but I was a terrible one. I was leading people down the road of hurt and pain and destruction—and I didn't even know it, at least not fully, until now. Now I was acutely aware of what I had done to myself and to others. My old attitudes and opinions had worked fine in theory, but I was going to need some new ones that would work in practice. I wasn't as smart as I thought I was.

I needed to learn more about these laws that I was breaking, these universal truths that I had been ignoring up to this point. But how could I figure it all out? Where could I go to learn more?

It turned out I was headed there next—deep in the heart of Texas.

Chapter 12:
Broken Faith

Noël came home at Christmastime and we continued to date. I loved her and didn't want to lose her, and she felt the same about me. By the middle of January, however, we had to leave each other again (although this time we would be only 1,000 miles apart instead of 8,000).

Noël was headed back to the U of I to finish her last semester of college, and I was headed to Houston, Texas, to start work in the computer department of the fifth largest corporation in America. The contrast from where I had been working in Dhaka and where I was going to work in Houston couldn't have been more dramatic. There were computers in both places but everything else was so different in Houston, from the sleek and shiny office building, to the aisles at the local Walmart. (Could the aisles at Walmart have been any wider or the shelves of groceries any higher? And how could any sane person really choose from so many different sizes and brands of ketchup?) Reeling from a bit of reverse culture shock, and adding to my lingering emotional shock, I began life again in Texas.

On the bright side, I had some relatives who lived in Houston, so I wasn't starting out all alone this time. The first week I was in town, my cousin Jane invited me to go to church with her to a large, 3,500-member congregation of some of the brightest and best-dressed people in the city. My cousin was part of a singles group made up of over a hundred young, single professionals who met every Sunday after the main church service. Although I had grown up going to church all my life, and had even gone to church while I was in college, I had never been part of such a big, dynamic church like this. The singles group alone was bigger than most churches I had ever attended. It was like a church within a church, complete with their own worship team and a message delivered by the full-time singles pastor.

Although I didn't know most of the songs, and I wasn't sure what to think about the people in the group, the very first message I heard the very first day spoke right to me. The speaker said there was a difference between "good depression" and "bad depression," that good depression can help drive us towards finding out what's wrong in our lives and how to change it. Even though I felt more than a little out of place at this church, I really wanted to come back and learn more.

I discovered the name of the singles group was called the Berean Class. I didn't know what a Berean was, so I asked my cousin. It turned out I *was* one! Jane showed me a verse in the Bible that described who the Bereans were: people who lived just after the time of Jesus in the city of Berea, in the country of Greece, and who wanted to learn more about Jesus. The Bible said:

"Now the Bereans were of more noble character than the Thessalonians, for they received the message with great eagerness and examined the Scriptures every day to see if what Paul said was true" (Acts 17:11).

The "Paul" mentioned here was at one time skeptical of Jesus—more than that, he killed those who followed Jesus—but he later became convinced that Jesus was the Messiah that the Scriptures promised would come someday to save the people from their sins. The people of Berea were like Paul at first, not sure if they could believe that Jesus was the promised Messiah, but they kept their hearts and minds open to the idea. They listened to Paul's messages with great eagerness, then examined the Scriptures daily to find out for themselves if what Paul said was true.

I *was* like the Bereans! Although I had been to church all my life, and I had liked a lot of things about it, I still had questions about some of the basics (like did God even exist?). It wasn't that I was against the idea of God, but I just wasn't sure if He really existed either. And I wasn't against the idea of Jesus being the Son of God, but I also wasn't sure if He was, or if He was anything other than a good teacher—or if He even lived or not. And whether He really lived or not, did it really matter? On two distinct occasions, when I had questioned these things before, the answers I got didn't make any sense to me.

The first occasion was when we were reading a passage from the Bible during a Sunday School class in junior high. In the passage, Jesus described Himself as the Son of God, saying:

"For God so loved the world that He gave His one and only Son, that whoever believes in Him shall not perish but have eternal life. For God did not send His Son into the world to condemn the world, but to save the world through Him. Whoever believes in Him is not condemned, but whoever does not believe stands condemned already because he has not believed in the name of God's one and only Son" (John 3:16-18).

As I read that passage, it sounded to me like Jesus was saying I had to believe in Him in order to go to heaven. I told my Sunday School teacher that I wasn't sure if I believed in Jesus or not, and if I was reading this right, then that meant I wasn't going to go to heaven when I died! She tried to assure me that I was a good kid and that I had nothing to worry about. But Jesus didn't say I would go to heaven if I was a good kid, but if I *believed* in Him! If having faith in Jesus was the key to heaven, then I knew I couldn't get in the door.

The second occasion that stumped me came not much after this when, at the age of thirteen, I took a class to join the church. I was glad to take the class and willing to join the church; but before I could join, I had to be baptized. We had the option in our church of being baptized as infants or baptized as adults, and my parents decided to let me make the decision on my own. It wasn't that they didn't *want* me to believe, they just wanted me to come to that conclusion on my own. In fact, my mom and dad were leaders in the church, they had taught my Sunday School classes at various times while I was growing up and they were leaders in a national organization to strengthen marriages and families, taking our whole family on a major trip every year to a national conference where every talk was about faith and marriage and family. So my parents were in no way indifferent to what I would decide—they just wanted me to make that decision on my own.

When it came time for me to join the church, however, and I was going to have to be baptized to do it—to publicly acknowledge my faith in Jesus in front of others—I didn't think I could do it. I understood it all intellectually, but I didn't believe in Jesus in my heart. On the day I was supposed to get baptized and join the church, I sat in a swivel chair in our living room, swiveling from side to side and trying to decide what to do. Some of my friends were going to join the church that day, and some of them were being baptized, too, but I didn't know if I could do it.

My family started turning out the lights to go to the car to go to the service—the service where they were going to watch me get baptized and join the church—and I still hadn't made up my mind. I don't know if it was the frustration of the moment, or the thought that I would eventually come to this conclusion anyway, but my parents gave me a little boost to help me along. They said that perhaps I could join now and keep growing in my faith as time went by. It sounded reasonable, and I decided to do it, even though I still wasn't sure what I believed about Jesus.

So when I discovered this class in Houston was called the Berean class—a whole class for people who questioned and wondered and eagerly searched the Scriptures to see if what the Bible said about God and Jesus and eternal life was true or not—I was happy to come along!

As the year progressed, Noël and I continued to see each other as often as we could. She would fly to Houston or I would fly to Illinois. We loved being together and hated having to say goodbye. We had no email, no Skype and our long-distance phone bills were becoming *huge*. So whenever we got together, we made the most of absolutely every minute, talking and laughing and being intimate as much as we could. Then we'd pull ourselves apart again and go back to our long-distance relationship. Whenever we were together, everything seemed so right. But whenever we were apart, I would start having doubts, questions and disturbing thoughts about our relationship again. I couldn't seem to *think* my way out of it, so I decided to *pray* to see if that could help me with some of my questions.

And God began to answer.

It began when spring came and the Berean Class held a weekend retreat at a place called *Camp Tejas* in LaGrange, Texas.

I loved being at the retreat. It reminded me of camping with my church and my family back home when I was a kid at a place called Woods Camp. Our days at Woods Camp were filled with running through the forest, cooking s'mores around the campfire and playing Four Square for hours using a ball and some chalk lines drawn on a concrete floor.

Now here I was, at the age of twenty-three, getting away for a weekend retreat and loving it again. This time, however, the spiritual component was much more front-and-center than the games we played.

The speaker for the weekend was dynamic. His face

beamed with light and excitement as he spoke. I was surprised and inspired to see someone get so excited about God. He talked about things that were relevant to my life at the moment, things like forgiveness (Jesus said to forgive people an *infinite* number of times—how was that possible?), friendship (Were we willing to pour ourselves into a few other people?) and patience (Why do we sometimes have to wait for God to answer our prayers? Is it because we aren't prepared for the answer or other people aren't ready or maybe God has something bigger in mind than we imagined?). Every topic touched on something in my life at that point.

When we divided up into small groups after one of the talks, the speaker asked us to tell each other who God was to us. Who was God to me? I didn't know. I started saying things I hadn't planned on saying and couldn't believe I was saying—they just came out of my mouth. I told them I wasn't sure if I really believed in Jesus, and I wasn't sure if He was the only way to heaven. I couldn't accept it; I had too many doubts. I was surprised to hear myself admitting these things out loud in front of all these people who seemed to believe wholeheartedly in Jesus. All my life I was "the religious kid," the one who went to church all the time. There was something freeing about finally being able to voice my doubts to others. Something must have been at work inside of me, helping me to face my doubts head on.

One of the guys in the small group invited me to study the Bible with him and several other men at a weekly Bible study that met at his home. It sounded like a great idea. I was glad to see what I could learn, as well as get to know some other guys. I agreed to come to his house later in the week.

Before the retreat ended, a woman stood up to say how special these retreats were to her because this was the first anniversary of when she put her faith in Jesus at the retreat the year before. I wasn't sure what to make of what she said. How could someone just decide one day to follow Jesus? What could possibly convince people that Jesus was real, causing them to commit the rest of their lives to following Him? How could anyone ever come to that conclusion, whether in a day or in a lifetime?

I was on my way to finding out for myself.

Chapter 13:
Breaking Up

The spiritual and the sexual sides of my life were both pulling on me hard. When I got home from the retreat on Sunday night, I went with a friend to see a movie that had just come out called *9-1/2 Weeks* (the *Fifty Shades of Grey* of the '80s). It was powerful, emotional and sexual. I loved it! I had just come off a spiritual high, and now I was getting a sexual high, too (but the contrast between the two events—the retreat and the movie—couldn't have been more pronounced!).

Noël was set to graduate the following Sunday, and she was planning to come visit me in Texas two weeks later. I couldn't wait to see her. I couldn't wait to be intimate with her. We had been doing this long-distance relationship for a year now, ever since my own graduation, always wanting and waiting to be together since we lived so far apart. And it looked like we were going to be doing the long-distance thing for a while longer.

Noël had been offered a job in Flint, Michigan, another 300 miles away from me. But since we were already flying back and forth to see each other anyway, another 300 miles wouldn't matter much, and she would get to work for a great computer company called Electronic Data Systems (EDS). Texas millionaire Ross Perot had started EDS with a $1,000 loan from his aunt the year before we were born. Just before Noël started working there, Perot sold the company to General Motors for $2.5 billion. So while I was working with computer systems at the fifth largest corporation in America, Noël was about to work with computer systems for General Motors, the first largest corporation in America. (Ironically, neither Noël nor I ever wanted to work in corporate America. We somehow just landed there.)

Noël's visit to Texas was still two weeks away. In the meantime I started studying the Bible with this group of about a dozen men on Wednesday nights. I wasn't exactly comfortable in the group, but it was nice to see how supportive they were of each other. I was even surprised to see these big, heterosexual guys crying with emotion during the prayer time, being so thankful for each other's support. I had never before seen anything like that.

I went back to the study again the following week, where we were reading from the Bible in what is called the book of John (because it was written by one of Jesus's followers named John). We were actually reading the passage that had stumped me back in junior high, the one in chapter three of John's writings where Jesus offered eternal life to anyone who would put their faith in Him.

At one point in the study, the leader of the group asked us all if we knew for sure that we would go to heaven when we died. I thought about my life, the things I had done and hadn't done, and I thought, *Yeah, I'm about 90% sure.* So when it came time for us to share our answers out loud, I shared mine first: "I'm about 90% sure."

Then I couldn't believe it when the guy next to me said he was 100% sure! *100%!?! Really? How arrogant!* I thought. *How can he be 100% sure what God's going to do with him when he dies?* Even though I had only started to get to know this guy, from what I knew, I thought that if anyone should be 100% sure, it should be me, not him! (Who was the arrogant one now?) Yet there he was, confident in his answer: 100%.

As the guys continued to answer around the room, every man said they were 100% sure: "100%," "100%," "100%," "100%," "100%."

Back to me: "90%."

The guy leading the study said to me, "Nick, the difference between 90% and 100% will change your life." The others agreed.

Was it true? I wondered. *Could people really know for sure what God was going to do with them when they died? Was it arrogant to put yourself in the place of God like that, or was that exactly what Jesus wanted us to know? Didn't He say that if we believed in Him we would have eternal life?* I voiced my questions out loud, and the guys showed me a similar verse in the Bible where John had written:

"I write these things to you who believe so that you may know *that you have eternal life" (1 John 5:13).*

Maybe Jesus really *did* want us to know for sure where we would go when we died. Maybe He didn't die so we'd be 90% sure we'd be saved. He died so we would *know* we would be saved. *Now that would give purpose and meaning to my life,* I thought, *if I really believed it.* But how would I ever be able to know for sure? I had no idea.

As spring turned into summer, Noël and I continued seeing each other whenever we could, loving each other more and more. Even though we were still so far apart, the distance seemed to draw us closer. I still had doubts about where our relationship was headed in the future, but I loved it for the present.

In August, I flew up to Michigan and spent a remarkable three-day weekend with her. It was the two-year anniversary of when we first started dating on our trip to the East Coast. Now it was two years later, and I couldn't have been happier than I was with her that weekend in Michigan. She had become the single-most important person in my life.

Noël showed me around her office building and showed me around her city, then we bought some food for a night of camping about twenty miles away in Holly, Michigan.

The whole weekend was glorious! We set up our tent and made a fire, then sat down to enjoy the beautiful view of the lakes and trees. The view of Noël was the best of all! Again, we outdid ourselves with our "I love you's," saying it to each other no fewer than 1,500 times that weekend. It felt so good to be together again, to hold each other and to be close. Noël was always so soft and playful and such a good friend. We walked under the stars and talked about work and life, and about the things we liked and the things we didn't like. We grilled hamburgers and sweet corn on the fire for dinner and cut up a fresh pineapple to go along with it. We ate as many Chips Ahoy cookies for dessert as we possibly could. Then we went to bed, zipped up together in our sleeping bags for a wonderfully intimate night.

I woke up the next morning with the sun, staring at Noël sleeping so peacefully next to me. I could have looked at her for hours. When she woke up, we started a fire and grilled bacon and eggs for breakfast. After eating, we took a walk through fields of wild flowers, which were tinted in every color imaginable. We rented a canoe and paddled out onto the lake, ending up in a swampy cove with reeds and cattails. We watched turtles sunbathing on logs, and we were surrounded by all kinds of butterflies and water life. A huge stork stood near us until we got too close, then it took off with a series of huge flaps of its wings. We rowed back to the beach where we returned the canoe, swam awhile, then promptly fell asleep on the beach—getting nicely sunburnt as we slept. We snuck into one of the campground showers together, slipped off our clothes, and had another romantic interlude.

When we got dressed again, we drove out to a blueberry farm nearby where the farmer let us pick and fill two gallon-sized buckets of blueberries. He said we could eat them while we picked, and I'm sure we ate as many as we put in the buckets. That was the first time Noël had ever tried blueberries, and she decided that she loved them (a big plus, in my opinion, as she was always hesitant to try new foods until she started traveling overseas). We grilled steaks on the fire for dinner and took pictures of each other in a field of flowers. Then we sat down on a blanket to watch the setting sun, talking again for hours, until it got dark and the stars came out.

I had never been more in love or more at peace with Noël than I was that weekend.

No wonder it came as such a shock to us both then, when three months later, I felt like God was telling me to break up with Noël.

Why God? I thought.

It was November, and I had just been to a spiritual renewal weekend at our church. The conference was one of the most powerful I had ever attended; I could practically feel God moving in my life. We sang worship songs and listened to talks about how God had worked so powerfully in each of the speakers' lives. Much of that weekend was focused on the activity of the Holy Spirit, and how the Holy Spirit was not just some kind of nondescript vapor, but was a Person who would actively guide, direct, correct and comfort us—as much as we were willing to let Him.

None of the speakers talked about dating relationships that weekend; no one told me to break up with Noël. Something just stirred inside me that weekend that I couldn't even explain. *Maybe it really was the Holy Spirit?* I wondered. All I knew was that by Sunday afternoon, I had the distinct impression that God wanted me to break up with Noël. Something wasn't right about our relationship, but I had no idea what. I loved her. She loved me. We absolutely loved being together. What could be wrong with that? And how could I possibly break up with her when I didn't even know *why* I was breaking up with her?

Yet I felt it so clearly—so strongly—that by Sunday night I called and broke up.

"Why?" she asked.

I had no idea. I didn't know what to tell her. I wished I

knew, but I didn't. All I knew was that I had to do it. There was no doubt in my mind; no second guessing.

This wasn't like me at all! I usually would have debated internally about a decision like this forever, especially one this significant. But I felt as if the Holy Spirit was pushing me in this direction—and I couldn't say no if I wanted to let Him guide me in my life.

I had been crying the whole weekend already, realizing that God really *did* have an active part in my life—and realizing that He would have an even bigger part in it if I would let Him. This was one of those first steps He wanted me to take, and I knew it. I knew this was going to be an "ebenezer" moment in my life, a touchstone that I would be able to go back to again and again to remember how God had been working in my life.

Noël didn't quite see it the same way! She couldn't understand why I was breaking up with her. It made no sense! *And if God wanted us to break up,* she thought, *then why hadn't He told her, too?* She was still convinced that God had spoken to her the very first day we met, saying, "That's the man you're going to marry." *How could our breaking up possibly be from Him?*

Noël cried for three days straight. Then pulling herself together in a way that only she could do, she came to the conclusion that if God wanted us to break up, then He must have someone better in mind for her. She told her friends that she couldn't imagine anyone better than me, but she knew she could trust that if this really was God who was taking me away from her, then He must have someone better in mind.

She was right. She was just going to have to wait a little longer to meet him.

Chapter 14:

Troubling Test

I was on the verge of a spiritual breakthrough. I could somehow feel it. At dinner one night with friends, one of them asked us all to describe our greatest spiritual experience. I said I didn't think I had had it yet, but I felt like it was coming soon —I just didn't know when or how.

Our weekly men's group was getting ready to start the new year by reading through the book in the Bible called Romans, which was named because it was written to the people living in Rome. Our group leader urged us all to get a good study Bible, a concordance and a Greek Interlinear. I had no idea what those last two things were, but I was wanting to get a new Bible anyway, so on January 2nd, I went to a local Christian bookstore and began to look around.

I found a thick, new study Bible that had come out a few years earlier called the *New International Version Study Bible.* The top half of every page contained an English language translation of the Bible, and the bottom half of every page contained additional footnotes that gave the history, background and definitions of the words in the passages above.

Then I found a massive *Strong's Concordance,* the biggest book I had ever bought in my life, containing an alphabetical listing of every word in the Bible, the location of each of those words in the Bible and the definitions of every word as found in the languages in which the Bible was originally written (Hebrew for the Old Testament, and Greek for the New).

Lastly, I found a Greek Interlinear Bible, which I discovered contained a line-by-line version of the New Testament with one line written in English followed by one line written in Greek (hence the name "interlinear") so someone could see exactly how each word was translated from the original Greek into English. I was more than a little intimidated as I walked out of the bookstore with a bag filled with these huge books, but I was eager to start looking through them. I really did want to seek God with all my heart.

As part of my own New Year's resolutions, I was also determined to spend my time differently that year. While Noël and I still talked from time to time on the phone, it was nothing like before, so I had lots of free time now to commit to some new habits. For starters, I decided to wake up an hour earlier and spend half an hour reading the Bible and half an hour praying, taking notes in a journal as I did. I also decided to read a Christian book for half an hour every night before going to bed. I picked out one by Charles Colson called *Loving God*. Not all of my goals were so spiritual: I hired a student from the local university to give me weekly swimming lessons at a local gym, and I made it a point to play the piano every day, something which I loved doing but never seemed to have enough time to do.

After buying my books, I began reading the Bible the next morning, starting with the book of Romans that we were going to be studying, and the book *Loving God* at night. I was instantly hooked by both.

Both books spoke straight to my heart—I couldn't believe it! I didn't realize the Bible had so much to say about sex, and about the loneliness that each of us feel that can only be filled by God. I was missing Noël, both physically and emotionally, yet I felt oddly good about it. Somehow it felt right. Being without her made me realize there was a bigger void in my life that she could never fill. Only God was big enough to fill it. I just never noticed the depth of that void since I was always trying to fill it with Noël.

As we began our weekly Bible study of the book of Romans, we started with a discussion of the first half of chapter one. Right in middle of chapter one, the topic started talking about sexuality—and not just sexuality in general, but about homosexuality specifically. I didn't know the Bible had anything to say about homosexuality, and I had never read any passage about it.

Romans talked about "the wrath of God." The topic of our discussion quickly turned to AIDS. AIDS was just starting to make the headlines at that time as the disease was beginning to spread exponentially throughout the gay community. Some people wondered out loud if AIDS was the wrath of God against homosexuals.

But as we looked closer at what the book of Romans said about God's wrath, I was surprised to read that God's wrath didn't often come in the form of raining fire and brimstone down from heaven onto us. God's wrath, the book of Romans said, was in "turning us over" to our own desires, letting us do whatever we wanted, and in so doing, we would "receive in ourselves" the natural consequences for our actions. God didn't *want* to destroy us! He wanted us to live! But if we persisted in doing what *we* wanted instead of what *He* wanted, He would let us follow our own way. *Free will* was one of His greatest gifts, as it allowed us to choose whether or not we would consciously love Him and those around us. While letting us choose a path that could possibly kill us had to be one of the hardest things God had ever done, it was also probably the most loving. Unfortunately, that also meant we wouldn't always choose what was best for us.

Most Disney villains seemed to die because of this, I thought. Even when the hero tried to show mercy to the villain, the villain usually did the wrong thing, doing himself in by taking a final swing at the hero then falling off a cliff to his death. The heroes usually didn't want the villains to die—and the heroes usually tried to save them. But the villains died when they followed their own path to its own logical conclusion. God was like the hero to us, showing us as much mercy as possible. But if we kept on swinging, we would eventually do ourselves in. God's wrath did not come by pushing us off the cliff, but by letting us choose whether or not we would take His hand when we were already falling off the cliff. If we didn't reach out and take hold of His hand, we would die of our own accord.

It was all beginning to make sense to me. What didn't make sense was that at one point during the Bible study that night, the Bible was talking about sin, and how everyone had sinned —how everyone had done something that went against what God wanted for his or her life. And the penalty for sin, the Bible said, was death.

I thought that was a little strong—death. I tried to think of any "sins" I had committed in my lifetime. I could hardly think of any for which I would get put in jail, let alone get the death penalty. I thought the Bible was being a little extreme. I shared my doubts about the whole concept of sin and death with the group. I didn't want to sound arrogant, I told the group, but I didn't think I had done anything for which I would ever get the death penalty. One of the guys in the group made a suggestion: "Nick, why don't you ask God what *He* thinks about how good you've been?"

I thought that was a fair question. If I had really done something for which I might possibly die, I would want to know about it. And if I hadn't, I would want to know that, too. Either way, I thought it would be good to know.

So when I went home that night, I began to pray to ask God what *He* thought about how good I had been.

But before I could get those words out of my mouth and into a prayer to God, I stopped. Did I *really* want to know the answer? What if I *had* done something for which I might die?

What if I *had* done something against God, and against *His* plan for my life, that I could *never* undo, that I could *never* take back—something which might eventually kill me as the natural consequences of my actions? Did I *really* want to know the answer?

I decided that I did. I wanted to know the truth. Either the Bible was true and what I believed was wrong, or what I said was true and the Bible was wrong. Both couldn't be true. I wanted to know the truth, so I asked.

Within two weeks God gave me my answer.

During those two weeks, another guy in the Bible study said he wanted to talk to me. He said he was worried about something in his life and wanted to talk about it, but was hesitant to do so. I wasn't sure what he wanted to talk about, but I wondered if it might have something to do with homosexuality. In fact, I hoped it did.

I was starting to have my doubts about everything I had been doing sexually. Since I had broken up with Noël, I had been having conversations with friends about God and sex and absolutes and prayer. I was beginning to wonder if maybe some of the things I had been doing sexually with her were wrong. I was beginning to see that doing what I desired for my life instead of what God desired for my life could end up making a huge difference in the way my life played out. I was opening up with my new friends in Texas about my sexual activity with Noël, but I hadn't told any of them about my sexual encounters with men. Earlier in that morning, on the very day that my friend called and said he wanted to talk, I had been asking God to give me someone with whom I could talk about my homosexuality.

When my friend called, I was so excited! God seemed to be already answering my prayers!

My friend and I got together the next day and we talked. My friend *did* want to talk about homosexuality. He said he had homosexual attractions for several years but had never acted on them. He didn't want to be gay, but he didn't know what else to do with his feelings. He said he had been growing closer and closer to God, like I was, and he felt like he wanted to clean up his life as much as possible as he said he cared about his relationship with God more than he cared about a relationship with a man. "Would you pray with me about all of this?" he asked.

I shared with my friend about my own sexual desires and activities, including my past homosexual encounters and how I had been wanting to get closer to God than to anyone else, too. Because I was talking so softly that night, my friend wondered if I really said what he thought I said. He couldn't believe it, as he had no idea I had ever been involved in homosexuality. He just wanted to talk! The more I talked, the more he realized I really had said what he thought I had said! I told him that even though it had been a couple of years since I had been with a man, I still had homosexual desires and attractions, even while I was dating Noël. Just hearing about how I had still dated Noël so passionately gave my friend hope that someday God might give him a woman with whom he could be passionate, too, regardless of his homosexual attractions.

He asked if I had ever been tested for AIDS. I hadn't. I hadn't even thought about it. AIDS was so new I didn't even know how it was transmitted exactly, other than it had something to do with homosexual activity. But now that he mentioned it, I wondered if maybe I should be tested. Maybe I did have it? I had heard that researchers thought that AIDS might lay dormant without symptoms for years. Maybe I had even passed it on to Noël without realizing it.

I started to become worried. What if this was just like the Bible had described, that God didn't *want* to kill me, but that there were natural consequences for going outside of His plan for my life, and those consequences *would* play out in my life. *I should probably get tested,* I thought. But that in itself was a scary thought! I usually passed out whenever I got a shot or had to have blood drawn. I wasn't keen on going anywhere to get stuck with a needle voluntarily, and I really didn't want to find out the results, either. But I knew it was probably a good idea. I thanked my friend for his concern and said I'd do it soon.

We talked some more and prayed, thanking God for our conversation. Even by just having this conversation with my friend, I could see God was already answering my prayers.

Chapter 15:

Total Surrender

As the week progressed, I decided to read the rest of chapter one in the book of Romans. I carefully reread the words again from the first part of the chapter that we had read the week before, and then I continued reading to the end of the chapter. I couldn't believe what I was reading! There, in black and white, was the answer to my question from two weeks before: I *had* done something that really could lead to my premature death. Here's what the rest of the chapter said:

"The wrath of God is being revealed from heaven against all the godlessness and wickedness of men who suppress the truth by their wickedness, since what may be known about God is plain to them, because God has made it plain to them. For since the creation of the world God's invisible qualities—His eternal power and divine nature—have been clearly seen, being understood from what has been made, so that men are without excuse.

"For although they knew God, they neither glorified Him as God nor gave thanks to Him, but their thinking became futile and their foolish hearts were darkened. Although they claimed to be wise, they became fools and exchanged the glory of the immortal God for images made to look like mortal man and birds and animals and reptiles.

"Therefore God gave them over in the sinful desires of their hearts to sexual impurity for the degrading of their bodies with one another. They exchanged the truth of God for a lie, and worshiped and served created things rather than the Creator—who is forever praised. Amen.

"Because of this, God gave them over to shameful lusts. Even their women exchanged natural relations for unnatural ones. In the same way the men also abandoned natural relations with women and were inflamed

with lust for one another. Men committed indecent acts with other men, and received in themselves the due penalty for their perversion.

"Furthermore, since they did not think it worthwhile to retain the knowledge of God, He gave them over to a depraved mind, to do what ought not to be done. They have become filled with every kind of wickedness, evil, greed and depravity. They are full of envy, murder, strife, deceit and malice. They are gossips, slanderers, God-haters, insolent, arrogant and boastful; they invent ways of doing evil; they disobey their parents; they are senseless, faithless, heartless, ruthless. Although they know God's righteous decree that those who do such things deserve death, they not only continue to do these very things but also approve of those who practice them" (Romans 1:18-32).

Those last words especially got to me: "Although they know God's righteous decree that those who do such things deserve death, they not only continue to do these very things, but also approve of those who practice them."

I had been active in many of the things on that list, including homosexuality. And even though I was no longer active in homosexuality, I still gave my full approval to those who were. When I read those final words of Romans chapter one, it was like a light went on inside my head. I could suddenly see that what I had done could quite literally lead to my death. I thought about the AIDS test I had said I was going to take. If the results came back positive, and I did have AIDS, it would not be because God wanted to destroy me, but because those were the natural consequences of following my own desires for my life instead of God's desires for my life. God didn't *want* me to die. He wanted me to live! But He had given me free will to choose to follow His plan for my life or follow my own.

I remembered back to the Bible stories I knew, about Adam and Eve and those first words God spoke to them: "Be fruitful and increase in number; fill the earth and subdue it" (Genesis 1:28a). God wanted us to live and produce life! But there was no way that I was ever going to produce life in a homosexual relationship, no matter how I matched up the parts. In fact, it was more likely to lead to my death, the very *opposite* of what God wanted for my life. I didn't want to die, and God didn't want me to die, but if I did die, I would simply be receiving the natural consequences for what I had done. That wasn't unfair of God. That was totally fair!

I suddenly felt terrible for what I had done, not just homosexually, but heterosexually with Noël, too. If I *did* have AIDS, I may have already passed it on to her! I thought I was just having fun. I thought I was just doing what I wanted to do because it felt good. But I hadn't given any thought to why God created sex, and what *He* wanted out of it, why He made it so pleasurable that we could hardly resist coming together to do it, and what He was hoping would come from my intimacy with another person. God loved life! God loved people! And He wanted the earth to be filled with them! So He created sex in a way that we would naturally be drawn towards one another, filling the earth with the people He loved! But the way I was using sex was never going to fulfill His purposes for creating it. In fact, that's one of the things I liked about homosexuality—I could have sex and neither my partner nor I would ever get pregnant! I didn't *want* to produce life. I just wanted the pleasure of it all. I felt like I had taken what God had given me and said, "I don't care!"

I had heard a story from our pastor at church a few months earlier, a true story about three men who went to confession one day. Two of the men convinced the third to make up a fake confession and tell it to the priest. The priest knew that the young man was lying, so the priest asked him to go to the altar, kneel down before a cross of Christ and say these words: "You did all this for me, and I don't give a damn!"

As the young man knelt at the altar, he couldn't bring himself to utter those words out loud. Instead, he broke down and wept, giving his life to Christ instead. The young man went on to become a priest himself. And that very man was the one who told this story to our pastor.

Now *I* felt like the young man in that story. I felt like I had taken this precious gift of sex that God had given me and I had used it for my own selfish purposes. I felt like I had already spoken those words to God, if not with my mouth, then certainly with my life, saying, "You did all this for me, and I don't give a damn!"

I was cut to the heart; pierced through as if with a knife. I was so sorry for what I had done, but I couldn't take it back. I couldn't take *any* of it back. I had already done it, and I was possibly already carrying the seeds of death within my body. If so, that was fair. God wasn't *against* me; He was *for* me. He was just as sorry for what I had done as I was. I was guilty as charged, and I knew it. There was nothing in the world I could do about it.

I wanted to take it all back. I wanted to change. But how? How could I change my thoughts, my feelings and my actions? I couldn't imagine anyone being able to change me: not my parents, not my friends, not a counselor.

But God hadn't finished speaking to me yet. There was more.

I got up and went for a walk that afternoon along the bayou in downtown Houston. I had my Bible with me, and I was reading from the book of Matthew as I walked. I came to a passage where two blind men came to Jesus. They wanted their sight back. They called out to Jesus as He walked along the road: "Have mercy on us, Son of David!"

I was surprised by what Jesus did next. Instead of touching their eyes or telling them to wash in a nearby pool, as He had done when He had healed others, Jesus asked them a question. Jesus asked:

"Do you believe that I am able to do this?" (Matthew 9:28).

In that moment, I felt like Jesus was asking me the same

question:

"Nick, do you believe that I am able to do this, too?"

I wanted to break free from the bonds that held me so tight, but I didn't know how to do it on my own. When I thought about Jesus and all He had done—how He had healed the sick, walked on water and raised the dead—I thought, *If anyone could do it, Jesus could!*

I stopped walking along the bayou. With my Bible in my left hand, I raised my right hand into the air. I looked up to heaven and said the same thing to Jesus that the blind men had said to Him:

"Yes, Lord, I believe."

And in that instant, I was healed—just like the blind men.

I knew I was changed. I felt as if an invisible atomic bomb had gone off inside me, with a blast that rippled all around the spot where I was standing. I didn't see anything happen with my eyes, but I knew it had happened in my heart. The power that held me was broken. I had been set free.

The next night I went to a class on world missions with my cousin Jane and her family. The speaker was talking about how Jesus came to die for our sins so we wouldn't have to. It was a message I'm sure I had heard throughout my life, but when you don't think you're a sinner, you don't think you *need* a Savior. That night I knew both. I was a sinner, and I needed a Savior, and Jesus was the only one who could save me.

As I listened to the speaker talk, I was enthralled. He summarized God's purpose for our lives, starting with the first book of the Bible, Genesis, to the last book of the Bible, Revelation. He told us how people had been turning their backs on God's desires and turning to their own desires instead ever since the earliest of days. As early as Genesis chapter six, things had already gotten so bad that God was seriously considering wiping out everything and everyone He had created. But God didn't *want* to destroy the world. He *wanted* us to live. So He spared Noah and his family because God saw that Noah was still righteous. God had mercy, and the world went on. But soon people were turning to their own ways again. God tried to woo them back—over and over throughout the Bible. But people kept turning against God.

The speaker compared God's plan in sending Jesus to what President Jimmy Carter had done during the U.S. hostage crisis in Iran a few years earlier. Some Iranians had taken fifty Americans hostage at the American Embassy in Tehran. Some people in the U.S. wanted President Carter to drop a nuclear bomb on Tehran—to blow the whole city to bits. President Carter said, "No, we need to get our hostages out first." Only then would he talk about what to do with the city.

Our world was like Tehran at that time. God has said He'll have to destroy our world completely someday, but He wants to get His hostages out first. So He sent Jesus to earth to warn us, to encourage us to turn away from our selfish desires and the certain destruction that would follow, to turn back to what God desires for our lives. If we would just put our faith in Jesus, God would forgive us of what we had done wrong so we could escape from the flames as the world was consumed. We couldn't get to heaven by any amount of good things we could do. We could only get to heaven by putting our faith in His Son, believing in Jesus for what Jesus had already done on our behalf.

Jesus didn't come just to tell us to love each other, the speaker said. We already knew that from the beginning. He came to save us from ourselves, to die for our sins, to die in our place so we wouldn't have to die.

I thought about what Jesus had done for me already, healing me the day before of my sexual bondage, the bondage that had a grip on me for so long. I knew I needed a Savior, and Jesus was exactly the kind of Savior I wanted, one who was willing to do anything for me—even give up His life so I could live.

I went home that night and couldn't believe it! Here was a man who loved me so much that He was willing to die for me so I could live. I had never felt so much love before in my life.

I wanted to call someone, anyone, but I didn't know who to call. I decided to call Noël. My love for her was the closest I had ever felt to this kind of love before. I wanted to talk to her. I went to the phone and picked up the handset, but before I could dial her number, I heard these words in my head:

"Talk to Me."

What? I thought. I wasn't sure what to do. I reached for the phone again. And again I heard these words in my head:

"Talk to Me."

What? I thought again. I reached for the phone a third time, and a third time I heard these words:

"Talk to Me."

This has to be God, I thought.

I put down the phone. I climbed onto my bed, got on my knees and planted my head in my pillow. Then I cried—deep, heavy, sobbing cries. I told God I was sorry for all that I had done in my life. I was sorry that I had made such a mess of it. I had been in control of my life for twenty-three years, and look what I had done with it. I wasn't in the gutter, I wasn't down and out, but I was headed in that direction. I was headed to death, and God wanted to put me on the path of life. I didn't want control of my life anymore. I asked Jesus to take control instead. I wanted Him to be my Lord, and no one else, not even myself. I wanted to blurt out the words, "Jesus is Lord!!" So I did.

At the end of it all, I was exuberant! I was exhausted! I thought to myself, *If I really believe this, I'll talk it through with someone else.*

Then I thought, *Wait a minute. Do I really believe this? Yes. Yes, I do. So who should I talk to?* My cousin Jane's parents came to mind—my dad's brother and his wife who also lived in Houston and with whom I had been talking the past few months, too. I knew they had been praying for me.

It was late at night—11 p.m.—and I wasn't sure if I should call them or not. What if I called them and then realized on my way over that I didn't really believe. Besides, I remembered that the speaker from the missions class was staying with them for a few days, as he had come to Houston from out of town. Maybe all of them would rather sleep, or talk to each other, and not to me. *No,* I thought, *they'd rejoice!*

My foot was off the bed, but I couldn't make it touch the floor. Somehow getting my foot to the floor was a step of faith I needed to take. I needed to step out in faith. I needed to put what I believed into action. I needed to put my foot down. So I did! I went to the phone and called my aunt and uncle, telling them I wanted to talk to them about my faith.

When I got to their house, I told them what I felt during the speaker's talk and afterward. I told them about the love I felt in my heart when I came home, about how I prayed to put my faith in Christ, giving Him control of my life. They were all so happy for me. I wanted to pray with them again.

I knelt down with my aunt and uncle and the speaker, all of us around the coffee table in their living room. We held hands and each of us prayed in turn, expressing everything that was on our hearts.

We closed our time of prayer by praying the Lord's prayer together, saying it in plain English as the words came from our hearts:

"Our Father in heaven, hallowed be Your name. Your kingdom come, Your will be done, on earth as it is in heaven. Give us this day our daily bread, and forgive us our sins, as we forgive those who sin against us. Lead us not into temptation, but deliver us from evil, for Yours is the kingdom, the power and the glory forever. Amen."

We hugged each other and thanked God for His answer to

our prayers.

I had one more question for the speaker. I told him I was afraid. I had read in the Bible that there would be persecution to come to those who profess Christ as their Lord. I was afraid of that kind of persecution, because it was described as extreme unto death.

The speaker said it was true, that persecution could come, but that God would give me His peace to endure it. Jesus called us to give up everything to follow Him—*but none of us could out-sacrifice God.* God had already made the ultimate sacrifice by sending His only Son to earth to die for us on the cross.

That was all I needed to hear. I was ready. I was willing. I was at peace. This was a call to total surrender, and I wanted more than anything to do it.

A woman in France in the 1600s, Madame Guyon, described surrender to God like this:

"...plunging your will into the depths of God's will, there to be lost forever."

I couldn't think of anything I would rather do.

I fell asleep that night on a bed at my aunt and uncle's house, with my eyes filled with tears and my heart filled with thanks.

The next day I woke up to a whole new life.

PART 4 ~ TAKING HOLD

Chapter 16:

Explosive Love

If I thought sex was the most explosive form of love, sex was nothing compared to the explosive love I felt when I put my faith in Christ. I couldn't have contained it if I tried.

I had already called my mom and dad and brother the night I put my faith in Christ—even though it was still in the middle of the night—to tell them about my newfound faith.

When I woke up the next morning, the first person I wanted to call was Noël. I had wanted to talk to her the night before—when God sovereignly interrupted me to talk to Him first—to tell her about this incredible love I felt in my heart. I was so thankful I talked to God first, but I still wanted to talk to Noël. She said she was glad for me and thankful I had made my decision to put my faith in Christ. But, like my mom and dad and brother, none of them quite knew what to make of it as I gave them so few details. I was just bursting to tell them about my decision.

But when I went to work that morning, the rejoicing started rolling in. My best friend at work, who had been going through this journey with me, and who was part of my weekly men's Bible study, said he had gone out for a drive the night before because he could tell something significant was happening. When he woke up in the morning, he knew it was going to be a beautiful, incredible day; he knew God was at work. He was blown away when he found out what had happened to me. My other friend from the men's group, the one who had confided in me about his struggle with homosexuality, was also ecstatic. He, too, sensed something significant was happening the night before, and he, too, had woken up in the morning finding *himself* fully recommitted to God—somehow feeling more fully aware of God's power and infinite glory than ever before. It was as if something had stirred in the world beyond ours, yet we were somehow able to sense it. Then I shared with yet another friend at work who had been talking and praying with me since we first met. He, too, was overjoyed.

Later that night, I shared what happened to me with a total stranger—a woman at a nursing home where I was visiting with some friends from church. The missions speaker from the night before had encouraged me to do this—to tell someone I didn't know about what I had done. So I did! I sat down next to this elderly woman and asked if I could share something special with her. I told her I had made a decision to follow Christ. She was so excited for me—even at the age of ninety—and asked me if I would pray for her. She said she wanted to be able to trust Christ even more in these final days of her life.

The joy kept flowing when the next night I went to my weekly men's Bible study and shared with them what I had done. They rejoiced even more than all the others! I got down on my knees in the middle of the room—along with my friend who had also recommitted his life to Christ—and we all thanked God for the work He had done in our hearts. None of the guys in our study knew about our struggles with homosexuality nor what God had done in our hearts regarding that topic; they were simply overjoyed with us that we had put our faith in Christ. I had gone from being 90% sure I was going to heaven to being 100% sure, and it had nothing to do with how good I was. It had everything to do with what Christ had done for me.

The singles pastor at my church heard about what I had done and asked me if I'd like to take fifteen seconds on the following Sunday to share with the class my good news. I said I'd be happy to (although I wasn't about to tell them about my previous struggles with homosexuality and, thankfully, I wouldn't have had time in fifteen seconds even if I wanted to). So after he spoke on Sunday, he asked me to come up.

I stood at the front of the room, shaking life a leaf, and looking out at the group of about 130 people. Many had already heard my news from earlier in the week, so they were already starting to clap and cheer for me before I said a word. Then I simply said, "I have some good news. I put my faith in Christ this week." They clapped all the more. I was so excited, I started clapping, too!

I kept shaking all over and said a brief prayer. A girl named Hayley came up to me afterward and told me this was the first day she had been back in any church for a long, long time. She said that my talk had convinced her that she had come to the right place, that she was "home," that this was exactly where God wanted her to be. She was gracious and kind and said she was truly touched by my testimony—even though it was only fifteen seconds long! Yet somehow that day marked the beginning of her return to church and to spending time again with other believers.

The explosion of love I felt inside was pouring out of me everywhere I turned. I've heard that if God is bigger than us, and He comes to live inside us, shouldn't some of Him show through us—so others can see Him? I felt like God was showing through me everywhere. I knew that any clapping or cheering or rejoicing was all for Him. It certainly wasn't for me —not with all that I had done! Any rejoicing had to go to Him who had *forgiven* me of all of that I had done.

Not everyone was happy about my newfound faith, however. When a friend from college came to visit me in Houston two weeks later, she said at one point during the weekend, "Nick, you talk about all kinds of things, but the conversation always seems to come back to God. I just want you to keep your perspective." She said it as an insult, but those words were like music to my ears! I *was* happy about my newfound faith, and I *was* thrilled about my new perspective! Everything *did* come back to God as far as I was concerned. When I talked to her again the following week, after she had returned home, she confessed to me that she had been thinking about God ever since we talked. She couldn't get Him out of her mind. I was thrilled again!

Then came the hard part. It was easy to tell people about my love for God. The hard part was telling them about my homosexual past.

I had to do it, though, and soon. I still hadn't been tested for AIDS, and I knew I really needed to do it. But even to ask someone *where* to be tested (there was no Internet back then to look these things up) was tantamount to confessing that I had been involved in homosexuality.

AIDS was still a very new disease, but it was starting to kill thousands of men in the U.S. right and left. Almost all of them were men who were involved in homosexuality, or who were intravenous drug users who shared their dirty needles with others. Given my fear of needles, anyone who knew me would know that I probably wouldn't have gotten AIDS from a dirty needle!

AIDS was still so new, in fact, that the word AIDS didn't even exist when I first went into homosexuality five years earlier. The word was coined in July of that year—one month *after* my first homosexual encounter. It was only two years before that when the Center for Disease Control even started tracking this disease that would later be called AIDS. And at that time, there were only thirty-one known cases of people who had died from it in the U.S., up to and including that year. By the time I was thinking about getting tested, five years later, over 16,000 people in the U.S. alone had already died from it. There was no cure. There was no hope. There were no drugs that could slow its inevitable progression towards death.

There was nothing popular, compelling or politically correct about the disease at that time. There were no fundraisers for AIDS research, no charity balls for AIDS awareness and no AIDS quilts for people who had died from AIDS.

Rock Hudson, the first "famous" person in the U.S. to die of AIDS, had died just eighteen months prior to the time when I was going to be tested—and the nation was still in shock from it. Homosexuality was actually still illegal in more than half the states in the U.S., including my new home state of Texas. You could be legally fired from your company or kicked out of your apartment or discharged from the military for simply admitting that you had been involved in a homosexual act. (And the president of the United States certainly wasn't going to call to congratulate you on your "courage" for coming out.) Even Rock Hudson never admitted that he contracted AIDS from homosexuality, a fact which came out only after his death.

But I had to find out where I could get tested for AIDS, and to do that I was going to have to ask someone for help—which would be, as I said, tantamount to telling them I had been involved in homosexuality.

There was a guy in our Bible study who was doing his residency at a local emergency room, so I decided to confide in him. I was petrified at the thought of it, but I sought him out and told him what I had done and what I needed. Thankfully, even though I didn't know him well, he showed me the Christian love and support I needed, and had hoped for, so badly. He told me about a clinic in Montrose, in the heart of the gay district in Houston, where I could get tested anonymously for $25.

The following week I went into the clinic, nervous to even walk through the front door, nervous to see the roomful of people who would all know why I was there, nervous because of my fear of needles and nervous for what the results might show.

Lovingly, God had put a woman in the clinic to help me. Her name was Ruby. I told Ruby about my fear of needles and my fear of the results. She had me lay back in a chair while she was drawing my blood in case I fainted, and asked me several questions about the types of homosexual encounters I had.

After telling her the things that I had done and not done, she said that I was in a low-risk category for contracting the disease, mainly because I had never "gone all the way" with anyone, male or female. The risk was still there, however, if there was ever a chance at all that I had gotten a cut or a tear in my skin or my mouth while being intimate with someone else where any exchange of bodily fluids might have taken place—no matter how brief. Who would have thought that such a brief moment of ecstasy could lead to such a deadly outcome?

Ruby's heart and her words helped reduce my fears, but I was going to have to wait another week for the results.

When I came back the following week, I was scared to death again for the first five minutes of walking into the clinic and waiting for someone to find my results. My fear eased when they told me good news: I didn't have AIDS.

Thank God, I thought. *Truly—thank God!*

I didn't know why I hadn't gotten AIDS, when so many others had. Some people complained that it was unfair when they found out they had AIDS, but for me that day, I felt like it was unfair that I *hadn't* gotten AIDS—when so many others all around me had. If I *had* gotten AIDS, I couldn't have blamed anyone else but myself. For whatever reason, I felt like God had given me a new shot at life, and I wanted to make the most of it.

Even though I loved my life before I put my faith in Christ —for I had been having a blast, working for a great company and traveling all over the world, having a great time—I never felt I had a *purpose* for living. Life was all about having as much fun as I could before it came to an end, and that was it.

But ever since the night I put my faith in Christ, I felt like I had a reason for living, a purpose that went beyond just enjoying life here and now. My purpose—in its broadest sense —was captured by a phrase I had heard and loved: *to glorify God and enjoy Him forever.* For me in particular, to glorify God meant to make His name known throughout the earth. And to enjoy Him forever meant to hang out with Him, do life with Him and do those things that both He and I could enjoy together. God wasn't going to *take away* my fun. He just knew that the way I was having fun could have killed me in the end—which neither of us wanted to happen. I had discovered my purpose for living the night I put my faith in Christ, and it was a purpose I could fulfill anywhere I went and at anytime. It wasn't dependent on whether I was married or single, working or unemployed or healthy or sick. Thankfully, now that my AIDS test had come back okay, I had more time than I thought to live out my purpose!

After walking out of that clinic that day, I was determined to make the most of my new life, no matter what the future held. Walking into church one morning, I saw an inscription on the cornerstone of the building that I had passed by many times before but had never really noticed. The words inscribed on the stone were now also inscribed on my heart:

"Man's chief end is to glorify God and enjoy Him forever."

That was the purpose of my life, and the purpose of all our lives if we're willing to take hold of it. I wanted nothing more than to fulfill that purpose.

Thank God, I thought again. *Truly—thank God!*

Chapter 17:

Power Broken

While I was experiencing my spiritual breakthrough down in Texas, Noël was experiencing her own up in Michigan.

My cousin Jane—the one who had invited me to church in Houston—had a friend named Julie who lived in Flint, the city where Noël was now living. Jane asked Julie to get in touch with Noël. The two of them connected and hit it off immediately.

Julie was the leader of a high school youth group in Flint and asked Noël if she could help out. Noël was glad to do it and started doing skits with the other leaders, telling jokes and throwing pies in each other's faces. Noël loved it, and the high school kids loved interacting with her.

Soon Julie asked Noël to give some of the weekly talks, which made Noël pretty nervous, but which made the students love her all the more. She talked to them about things like self-esteem, faith, dating and relationships. Noël had recently bought the same *NIV Study Bible* that I had bought, and she found herself learning more about the Bible—as she was now trying to teach from it—than she had ever learned when she was listening to other people talk about it.

About two weeks before I put my faith in Christ, Noël went with Julie's youth group to see a Christian singer named David Meece. David was funny, deep and a great singer and pianist. All the words he spoke and the songs he sang seemed to express everything Noël was feeling about life and God at the time. Noël especially loved David Meece's song, *We are the Reason:*

"We are the reason that He gave His life
We are the reason that He suffered and died
To a world that was lost, He gave all He could give
To show us the reason to live"
Noël was learning that God had purpose for her life, too. By the end of the concert, when David invited anyone to come forward who wanted prayer or to make a deeper commitment to God, Noël wished she could stand up and go to the front. She was eager to follow God anywhere. She had always been thankful that God had given her life, and she had always felt He had been there for her whenever she needed Him. Although she wanted to go forward at the end of the concert, this was all still so new to her that she wasn't sure what to do. So she stayed in her seat, and right there she made an all-out commitment to God, finally giving Him complete control of her life.

Noël had always considered herself a Christian, having always believed in Jesus ever since she was a little girl. (She had even wished that she could marry Jesus someday, if that were possible.) But Noël had never made Jesus the *Lord* of her life, giving Him *complete* control, which she finally did that night.

Back at the weekly youth group, Noël started facing some new challenges as she tried giving God control of her life in this new way. She had already started dating some of the other guys who were helping to lead the youth group, but now she discovered that the physical boundaries she had set up for her relationships in the past were no longer working. Some of the guys wanted to go farther with her than she had gone before. She didn't want to, and for the first time she began to wonder if she had already gone farther than God wanted her to go. The sexual touching she had felt so comfortable with in the past somehow seemed uncomfortably wrong to her now. She had seen the hurt and pain that it caused to others, and she was starting to feel the hurt and pain of it herself.

One of the leaders she was dating had been intimate with her one night, leading her to start putting her hopes and expectations in their relationship. But the day after they were intimate—and for several weeks thereafter—he completely ignored her. *What was going on?* she wondered. *What were these guys possibly thinking!* Her conclusion: they weren't! They were just doing what felt good to them.

Noël always justified her sexual intimacy by thinking that God wanted her to be happy, and since sexual intimacy made her *really* happy, God must be all for it. But now she was beginning to realize that while God *did* want her to be happy, He had designed sexual intimacy in a way that worked best in the context of a committed relationship for life—marriage. Without that commitment, there was way too much room for hurt and pain—or worse. (As Billy Graham once said: "Sex is the most wonderful thing on this earth, as long as God is in it. When the Devil gets in it, it's the most terrible thing on earth.")

Noël was wanting to let God direct her life—every aspect of it—including her sex life. She wanted sex to be the most wonderful thing on earth, and that meant changing what she did with the guys she dated.

Although I wasn't dating her any more, I still loved her and cared about her deeply, and we still talked on the phone from time to time. When she told me she had started dating some of these guys, it scared me. Part of it could have been the pangs I felt for not being able to be with her myself, but part of it was because I was truly afraid for what might happen to her in the hands of someone else.

I was especially scared for her during those weeks when I was wondering if I might have AIDS. What if I *did* have AIDS and I had somehow passed it along to her? What if she was now passing it along to these other guys by being intimate with them? I didn't want to worry her by telling her about my fears —because I still had no idea at that time if I had AIDS or not.

And I didn't want her to think I was trying to manipulate her new relationships by telling her what to do or what not do with these other guys.

But after I put my faith in Christ, and after I finally received the results of my AIDS test, I sat down and wrote Noël a long, long letter. I shared, in detail, why I had decided to follow Christ, my fear of dying and my thankfulness for receiving the gift of eternal life. It felt glorious to finally be able to share with her the fullness of what had happened inside of me. Since she was going through a similar experience herself with God, she seemed to truly understand what I was saying. She called to tell me about her own commitment to follow God in a new way as well.

Having opened up to a few people now about my AIDS test (including my friend who encouraged me to get tested, the doctor who suggested where to get tested and now Noël), I began to open up to a few more of my close friends about my past sexual experiences with both men *and* women—and exactly what God had saved me from.

I nervously told my best friend at work about my homosexual past, fearing that it might destroy our great friendship. He responded with amazing loving-kindness. Rather than pulling back from me, at the end of our conversation he gave me a hug! It's hard to express the overwhelming emotion I felt at that moment, when I feared for the worst and he gave me the best—exactly what I needed—his understanding and acceptance, encapsulated in a hug. He said he had never had any of the thoughts or feelings that I had shared with him, but he was thankful that I trusted him enough to tell him about it. That one hug from one solid, heterosexual guy began to undo a lifetime of hurt I had received from those who had ridiculed me in the past.

Next, I went out to a park with my cousin Jane for a picnic lunch. Nervous again, and while we were sitting on a blanket on the grass and eating sandwiches, I shared with her, too, about my past. Again, I was blown away by the response. Jane didn't condemn me or freak out on me or think I was the equivalent of an axe murderer. Instead, she responded with grace, compassion and much wisdom. I asked her if she thought I should keep telling others my whole story, including people like my mom and dad and others who were close to me but who didn't yet know.

I told her I was afraid but willing to do it if that's what God wanted me to do.

Jane's response was full of wisdom. She said that while God wanted us to speak the truth, He also wanted us to speak the truth in love. It was important, she said, to make sure that whatever I shared, I shared it in love, telling others what would be most helpful to them. She pointed out that even Jesus held back at times from telling His disciples *everything* He knew because He knew it would be more than they could yet bear. At one point, Jesus said to them:

"I have much more to say to you, more than you can now bear. But when He, the Spirit of truth, comes, He will guide you into all truth" (John 16:12-13a).

Jesus had much more He could have said to them, but He knew it would be better at a later time. While the truth *is* good, truth needs to be spoken in love—at the right time and for the right reasons. Jane's advice helped guide me along as I continued to pray about who to tell and when.

When the pastor of the singles class asked me if I would share my full testimony with the class one day that summer, I had a different reason for holding back: I knew *I* was the one who wasn't ready for that yet. The toll on me would have been too much, as I was so new in my faith. I knew I had a lot more growing to do before facing that kind of public exposure.

It was perhaps because of my cousin's advice that whenever I did feel prompted to share my whole story, those I shared it with responded better than I could have ever expected. My sharing almost always caused people to rejoice with me at my changed life—and to deepen their own commitment to following Christ with their whole lives.

One of the most surprising things to me on this new side of my faith commitment was that my feelings, attractions and desires towards men had changed almost entirely, too. It was as if God had turned off a huge electromagnet that had once been surging through my body. Men who had previously been disturbingly attractive to me were now almost entirely neutral. I say "almost" entirely because I still recognized a handsome man when I saw one. But that magnetic pull to want to be with them, physically or romantically, had dissipated.

This was most apparent to me when a guy from the Berean Class asked me out to lunch one day. He was incredibly handsome: tall, blonde and well-built, with soft blue eyes and a chiseled chin. Before I put my faith in Christ, I had a hard time even carrying on a conversation with him for fear that I might stare at him too long.

But now, sitting with him at lunch for a whole hour, I was amazed how all of those feelings of physical and emotional attraction were gone! He was still as handsome and good-looking as before, but that magnetic attraction was replaced by a simple appreciation for his heart, for his life and for the conversation at hand. We hung out together several times over the weeks that followed, going for coffee or to the Houston Rodeo. Each time I was amazed at how much my feelings and desires had changed.

Perhaps it was my brush with death—and the new realization that homosexuality could be, in fact, harmful to my health—that kept my feelings and attractions at bay. But the healing I felt inside me seemed to go much deeper than just the fear of death. Jesus had somehow broken the grip that homosexuality had once had on me. And the more I revealed

my personal struggle with homosexuality to people—especially
with people who had no interest in me sexually—and I found
they still accepted me and loved me just as much as before,
those attractions and desires faded away even more. Were those
thoughts, feelings and attractions all gone? No, but I had
started to realize that what I really wanted in my relationships
with men was acceptance, mutual care and concern. Now that I
was getting that legitimate need fulfilled in other ways, I no
longer felt the need to try to fulfill it in illegitimate ways.

As the summer went on, I began to take more notice of
some of the beautiful women in the Berean Class, wondering if
God might still have a woman in mind for me with whom I
could spend the rest of my life. Other than Noël, I hadn't really
had a strong sexual attraction to any other women. I began to
date a bit, going out with one or two women in the class. They
were sweet and fun, and I loved our outings and our
conversations, but nothing clicked with them quite like it had
with Noël.

One woman, however, captured my attention more than the
rest. I tried to keep a healthy distance from her, though,
because it was Hayley, the woman who had come up to me
after I shared my fifteen-second testimony in front of the class.
She was beautiful, she was spiritual and she always seemed
genuinely glad to see me. But she was just starting to come
back to church and be around other believers, so I didn't want
to do anything that might push her away from that. Yet she was
truly attractive to me, both inside and out.

Every time we talked, we couldn't help but get excited
about all the things that God was doing in our lives. We started
running into each other more, so we continued talking, praying
and sharing our lives more and more.

One afternoon, Hayley came over to my apartment. We sat
down on the floor by the couch to talk, then our eyes met.
Suddenly we stopped talking. All I wanted to do was lean over

and kiss her lips. I could tell she wanted the same. I took a deep breath, and decided to tell her what I was thinking. "I'd love to kiss you. Would that be okay?" I asked.

To my delight, she smiled and said, "Yes."

I leaned over and kissed her on the lips. Then I kissed her some more (and some more), loving every minute of it.

I could feel myself getting aroused. I knew I wasn't going to be able to keep going like this much longer and still keep my commitment to sexual purity at the same time. I felt like I was in a car, pressing on both the gas pedal and the brake pedal at the same time.

Unable to take it anymore, I finally had to pull back from our kisses. I took another deep breath, and just looked into her eyes. That did about as much for me as all the kissing had done before!

The room was suddenly much hotter than I remembered, and the physical effects of my arousal were more apparent than I wanted them to be. We stood up to say goodbye, but the shorts I was wearing did little to hide my obvious arousal. I apologized. She wasn't fazed. She looked at me with her dark brown eyes and said it was fine, not to worry about it at all. We kissed one last time and said goodbye—with a smile on my face and with my blood still rushing to more than just my cheeks.

As embarrassed as I was, I couldn't help but think that God might still have a woman in mind for me after all.

Chapter 18:

First Fast

Hayley and I continued to date for several more weeks. While I had to pull back from kissing her at all in order to keep our physical purity intact, we still enjoyed romantic outings, home-cooked meals, foot massages and extended times of praying and reading the Bible together. (While praying and reading the Bible together might not sound very romantic to some people, there's nothing more powerful than having a strong heart connection with God and with someone else at the same time. A couple once told me that on their honeymoon they prayed every night together just before falling asleep. "There's nothing more intimate," they said—and I could understand why.)

I loved getting closer to God and closer to Hayley. I also kept hanging out with my friends from work and my friends from church, and I still talked at times on the phone with my friend Noël.

One night while talking to Noël on the phone, she told me that she was trying to decide what to do about her job. The company for which she worked, EDS, had one of the strictest policies in the computer industry for retaining their employees after sending them through an intense training program. Their training was so good that other companies would often try to hire EDS employees away from EDS after giving them what was called their "Phase II" training. In an attempt to ward off talent scalpers from stealing their best employees, EDS required anyone who went through their Phase II training to sign a letter of agreement stating that they wouldn't leave EDS for three years afterward—or pay a penalty of $10,000 if they did.

Noël was getting ready to start her Phase II training in a few months, at which time she was going have to sign the letter of agreement. The company could then send her anywhere in the world and she would have to keep working for them for at least three years, no matter what, or pay the $10,000 penalty. Noël didn't know what she should do.

I could tell this weighed heavily on her heart. She had a great job with a great company, but she wasn't sure if this was what she wanted to do for the rest of her life or even for the next three years.

I had been reading in the Bible about the topic of prayer and fasting and how people who prayed *and* fasted seemed to have closer conversations with God—and more effectiveness in their prayers. I had wanted to try praying and fasting for myself, so I told Noël I would try it the following week and that I would pray for her job decision while I did. I was glad we had kept in touch as I was excited to see how much closer to God both of us were now growing.

On Monday of the following week, I began my first-ever fast. I had read about different kinds of fasting and had decided I wanted to give up all food for five days, drinking only water and fruit juice during that time. The first day was uncomfortably hard. My body rebelled against me for not feeding it. My stomach kept sending its "Feed me!" signals to my brain, making me feel lightheaded. Instead of thinking more about God, all I could think about was food!

But by the second day, my body had already adjusted. Realizing that no food was going to be coming its way anytime soon, my stomach stopped sending its protests to my head. I decided to take the day off work so I could focus more clearly on my prayers.

It was a beautiful, sunny day in Houston, so I went outside

to sit by the community pool in the middle of my apartment complex. With my Bible open on one side of me, and my prayer journal open on the other, I sat down on a reclining pool chair and began to pray. I prayed for everything that was on my heart, including Noël's job decision.

As I was praying for Noël, I began to think about her office where she worked. I could still picture her from my trip to Michigan, all dressed up in her business clothes, working with computer programmers and systems analysts throughout the day. With that picture in mind, I felt like something didn't seem right about it. I could picture her more in a pair of blue jeans and an oversized sweatshirt, working with kids or staying at home and raising a family. She was smart and she could obviously do well in corporate America if she wanted, but that just didn't seem like the best fit for her.

What she really needs, I thought, *is a husband! If she had someone who could take care of her, not in a demeaning way, but in a way that allowed her the freedom to do whatever God put on her heart to do, that would be so much better for her.*

That's it! I thought! *Noël doesn't need a new job! What she needs is a husband!*

So I began to pray that God would give her a husband. As soon as I did, these words came into my head:

"Why don't you marry her?"

What?!?! I thought. *That wasn't what I was expecting at all!* This couldn't possibly be from God (could it?). I mean, wasn't God the one who told me to break up with Noël the year before? Why would He now be asking me, "Why don't you marry her?"

I must be delirious! I thought. *This fast must be affecting my head.*

It wasn't that I didn't love Noël. I did—incredibly! It was just that God had been so clear with me the year before that He wanted me to break up with her. I couldn't understand why He would suddenly want me to get back together with her? Not to mention the fact that I was happily starting to date

Hayley, who was perfectly lovely, godly and all-around wonderful.

This couldn't possibly be from God. I closed my eyes, closed my Bible and closed my journal. I laid back in my recliner chair and tried to clear my mind so I could pray about something else.

By the end of my five-day fast, I couldn't believe how much better I felt. I was more energized and more refreshed than before. Other than having that odd episode of thinking I heard God asking me that question about marrying Noël, the fast had been a compelling exercise, and I hoped to do it again sometime.

But two weeks after my fast ended, I still couldn't get that question out of my mind: "Why don't you marry her?"

Maybe I wasn't thinking right about the question. Maybe God was saying, "Why *don't* you marry her?" God had never given me a good reason why He wanted me to break up with Noël. Maybe He wanted me to keep praying about it so I could discover why I *didn't* marry Noël, so I could go on with my life without her.

But that didn't really make sense either. God had already shown both Noël and me a number of reasons why He wanted us to break up: first and foremost was that neither of us had made an all-out commitment to Him, and second, we were doing things with each other sexually that we shouldn't have been doing without a commitment of marriage between us.

Maybe God wanted us to break up long enough so we could get our focus on Him? And now that He had our full attention, maybe He wanted to bring us back together again. Could it be that God really *did* want me to marry Noël? Was God *really* going to give her back to me, and me to her, after all?

I didn't know what to think. I didn't know what to do. And what about Hayley? I liked her—a lot! She was always fun and encouraging and I loved being around her. From the day we first met, it seemed like God had put us into each other's lives to boost our faith in Him. Maybe we could still do that without dating, but it seemed just as likely that we could do it as a couple, too. I needed more time to think and pray about it all. But how could I pray about possibly marrying Noël while I was still dating Hayley? I knew I couldn't.

If I was going to pursue this question any further, I was going to have to break off things with Hayley—at least for a while. I decided the best thing to do would be to tell Hayley the truth—tell her what had happened during my fast, and tell her that I needed to resolve this question in my mind before dating her any further. It was a huge risk, and I felt bad for Hayley. Who would want to be set aside for a period of time while the person you were dating was praying about marrying someone else? But, on the other hand, who would want to be dating someone when the person they were dating was praying about marrying someone else!? It would be better for everyone if I backed off dating anyone for a time. So I decided to talk to Hayley.

I told her what had happened on my fast. I told her I had no idea if God was speaking to me or not, but I needed to find out. I suggested that we take three months off of dating each other so I could focus on this question as best I could. Three months seemed like enough time for me to hear from God more clearly—and if I heard nothing more in three months, I could write it all off as food deprivation.

I was afraid Hayley would be upset, but she responded with grace and understanding. And, as always, she only wanted what God wanted above all else. We had already stopped kissing (practically as soon as we had started), which made this transition much, much easier.

As I began to pray about Noël, God did something incredible in my heart: He put a love in my heart for Noël like I had never had before. All of a sudden, I wanted to talk to her, be with her, pray with her and be intimate with her all over again, but even stronger than before!

I knew I couldn't do any of those things, not yet. I told myself when I started this three-month period of prayer that I wouldn't say anything about it to Noël. I had already put her through one horrific heartbreak when I broke up with her the first time, and I didn't want to put her through two. Plus, I wanted to keep my thoughts as clear as possible so I could hear from God first—without the distraction of talking to Noël more often than usual.

I did tell her, though, that I had prayed for her during my fast, and I told her that I had prayed God would speak to her about her job. In my heart, however, I started going over and over all the things I loved about Noël and what it would be like to be married to her one day.

I got to see Noël once during that three-month period, when we were both back in Illinois for Thanksgiving weekend. Noël came down to meet me at our farm on a Saturday afternoon. We took a long and very memorable walk down the country road near our house. I had never seen *anyone* look as cute in my life. She was wearing her faded, oversized jean jacket and the sun was highlighting the curls of her hair. She had her hands in her jacket pockets, and she smiled and laughed as we walked along the road. The way she walked, it looked like she was dancing. Inside, I was dancing, too!

When I got back from that walk, all I knew was that I wanted more than anything to marry this girl. I flew back to Texas, and Noël flew back to Michigan—and my heart was once again overflowing with love.

I hadn't forgotten about Hayley, of course, and I knew I needed to tell her what God was doing in my heart. It seemed that God really had been speaking to me during my fast, and I wanted to let Hayley know what He was saying before too much time passed. I told her what was going on, and to my surprise, she felt like this was the right thing for me to do, too. She had met Noël on a previous visit and always thought we were perfect for each other. I appreciated her sincere understanding, and I was now able to concentrate on praying for Noël without reservation.

On the final day of my three-month period of prayer, I decided to call Noël. I didn't know what I was going to say exactly. I just knew I wanted to tell her what God had been doing in my heart. Although I still didn't have a "final" word from God about whether He wanted me to marry her or not, I knew what *my* vote would be! I was all in. If Noël would have me, and God would confirm that this was really from Him, I wanted more than anything to marry her. (And if God *didn't* let me marry her, I was going to be so mad!)

I called Noël several times that day, but couldn't get a hold of her, so I left a message asking her to call me back. I had to trust that God had it all under control.

When she called me back the next day, I asked her how she was doing.

She told me she had finally made a decision about her job. She didn't think she could sign the letter of agreement, so she planned to keep working up until she had to sign it, then she was going to quit. She was sure this was the next step she was supposed to take, but she had no idea what she was going to do after that.

I told her I had an idea:

"What would you think about moving to Houston and praying with me about getting married?"

Now Noël was the one who went into shock!

Chapter 19:

Heart's Desire

Noël couldn't believe it! She had always loved me and had always wanted to hear this from me! She had even prayed when we broke up that one day I would come to love her like this and ask her to become a permanent part of my life. When we broke up, she trusted that God would give her someone better than me. And now He had! I was *way* better than the old Nick, now that I had put God first in my life. Noël was amazed— amazed at God, amazed at me and amazed that God had answered her prayers, even her prayers from so long ago.

But Noël was also wisely cautious. After I broke up with her, she didn't know if she could *ever* marry me. While she had hoped this would happen, she wanted to be sure about it all before we actually got back together. She wanted to think and pray about it, but she was definitely excited at the thought of it.

I totally understood her caution, and I totally expected and appreciated it. I couldn't have asked for more. I was just so thankful that I was finally able to express to her all the love that had been building up inside my heart. Whatever happened, I knew God would speak to us if He really wanted us to be together.

Noël called again two days later and asked if I would come up to see her in Michigan the following weekend. She was going on a ski trip as a leader with the junior high youth group from her church, and she wanted me to come along.

I thought it was too soon. I wanted her to pray about it more before we saw each other again, so she could hear from God more clearly. But she wanted me to meet her new friends, to see what she was doing with her life and to make sure this was really what I wanted, too. She was worried that I might have idolized her while we were apart, and she wanted to make sure I really did want to get back together again. I knew nothing she would do that weekend would change my desires for her, so by the end of our conversation, I suggested that maybe we had better wait. Noël was hurt and disappointed.

I could tell this was really important to her—so that made it important to me. The more I thought about going to see her that weekend, the more I was able to see it through her eyes. She needed to see for herself that I was really serious about this. I had hurt her before, and I needed to do more than just talk to gain back her trust. I called her back and told her I'd love to come.

Noël said the very words that I had been thinking in my heart: "Thank you for seeing it through my eyes." That was the confirmation I needed to go through with it, even if I felt like it was too soon.

I flew up to Michigan that weekend and fell deeper and deeper in love with Noël. She had always been cute, but that weekend she was gorgeous, both in body and in spirit.

I loved watching her as she laughed with her friends, did skits for the kids (dressing up as a dwarf with her ears poking out of her hoodie) and encouraged everyone she encountered in their faith. She was everything I had pictured and more.

On Saturday night, when we finally had a chance to talk on our own, we went upstairs in the old Victorian hotel where we were all staying. Noël and I sat down in the hallway to talk. She started telling me what she had been thinking about everything I had said.

She said that as much as she wanted to get back together with me, she felt like this was the first time in her life that she was getting to live life on her own. She liked her new life and her new independence. She was growing deeper in her faith, making great friends and loving working with the kids at the church. She said she was really sorry, but she wasn't ready to give that all up.

I was sad—crestfallen, as much as anything. My bubble of excitement had burst, but I understood.

I felt like Jim Carey in the movie *Bruce Almighty,* when his character, Bruce, asked God:

"How do you make somebody love you without affecting their free will?"

"Welcome to My world, son," God replied. "You come up with the answer for that, and we'll talk."

There was nothing more I could say to Noël. She thanked me for coming to see her, said goodnight and without a goodnight kiss or any indication that she ever wanted to get back together again, she stood up and walked away.

I sat on the floor and cried.

I had my Bible in my hands, so I opened it up and started reading through a few of the Psalms. When I read Psalm 20 and got to verses four and five, I cried again—but this time with joy. The Psalm said:

"May He give you the desire of your heart and make all your plans succeed. We will shout for joy when you are victorious and will lift up our banners in the name of our God. May the LORD grant all your requests" (Psalm 20:4-5).

God had already given me more than I could possibly ask for from Him. He had forgiven me of my sins, He had given me a new life here on earth and He had given me the promise of eternal life with Him. I knew I had already gotten way more than I deserved, so how could I ask Him for more?

But when I read those words, I was encouraged and wanted to ask Him for one more thing. While I didn't want to sound ungrateful on the one hand or extravagant on the other, I also knew that God still had more for me on this new path of life on which He had put me.

Not knowing if Noël would ever say, "Yes," I underlined those verses from Psalm 20 in my Bible. I told God that night that if I could ask Him for just one gift in my entire lifetime, it would be to marry Noël. I knew it may have sounded childish, but I was serious. I prayed with all my heart that night that God would give me Noël. Then all I could do was wait.

I flew back to Houston, and Noël kept working for EDS until she began her Phase II training. When the time came for her to sign her three-year agreement, she resigned. She stayed in Flint a little longer, then moved back to Illinois for the summer to work at a camp for kids with disabilities.

Noël loved the idea of helping others, like Mother Teresa was doing in Calcutta, and this was the perfect time in her life to try it full time. She spent each week at the camp living in a cabin with a different group of girls, helping them eat, changing their clothes, giving them showers, playing games with them and reading to them from the Bible. We continued to talk during all of this, and I was so proud of her for doing what she really felt she should do. She said it was the hardest, most rewarding summer of her life.

At the end of the summer, Noël went with her youth group to a week-long camp in Colorado, then flew to San Francisco to be in a friend's wedding. She called me from San Francisco to tell me about her friend's wedding and how happy she was that the bridesmaid's dress she was supposed to wear fit her so well. I asked her to send me a picture, and she said, "Oh, I'll just bring the dress with me when I come to Houston."

"You're coming to Houston?" I said.

"Of course I'm coming to Houston!" she said.

I couldn't believe it! She said she had *always* planned on coming to be with me in Houston in the fall, once she quit her job at EDS and did some things that she had really wanted to do that summer. She wondered why I sounded so surprised, as she said she had told me before! I didn't know if this was just her way of getting back at me for breaking up with her, or if she didn't want to give away too much of her heart before she was ready, or if she really had told me and *somehow* I had missed it. (*Somehow* I think I would have noticed that she said she was coming!) Whatever the reason, it didn't matter! All that mattered was that she was really coming!

Oh, God! You really do answer our prayers! I thought.

So that fall, Noël packed up her things and moved to Texas. I talked to my aunt and uncle, and they said Noël could stay with them while she looked for an apartment of her own.

She filled out an application to work in the computer department at the same company where I worked, in the same building, and they called her back after the interview to say they were happy to hire her.

For the first time in three and a half years, we were finally living in the same city again. We got to see each other at work and in the evenings after work—every single day! We began praying together that God would give us His final okay to get married, hoping that this had been His plan all along.

About a month into our prayers, Noël was starting to get impatient with God and with me. She was ready for an answer. She had made her decision, and I had already made mine, and she wondered why we were waiting on God for something more.

For Noël, the last five minutes of a road trip were always the worst. She was fine all the way up until those last five minutes, then she just wanted to *be there*. Noël's sudden impatience was like an indicator that we were almost there—and we were!

My answer came on a Saturday morning, November 19th. We had gotten up early that day to watch one of our friends run a race in the Galleria area of Houston. After the race, Noël came back to my house where we were going to spend some quiet time with God before going on with the rest of our day, as we were both now in the habit of doing.

I went to my bedroom to read my Bible and pray, and Noël stayed in the living room to do the same.

I sat down on the floor and opened my Bible, not knowing what I should read. I had just finished reading the entire Bible from cover to cover a few days before for the first time in my life, and I didn't know where to start reading next. So I started again from the beginning.

As I opened to Genesis chapter one, I read how God created the earth and filled it with all kinds of plants and animals. I had heard the story many times in my life, but this was the first time I saw it from God's perspective.

I tried to imagine what it must have been like for God, to look down on His beautiful creation, filled with all kinds of plants, animals and the first man, Adam. God put Adam in the Garden of Eden to work the ground and take care of the garden. In the midst of this incredible paradise, the Bible said that Adam was all "alone." There was no one like Adam with whom he could truly share his life and do his work. I could imagine how sad God must have been when He saw that Adam still felt all alone.

So God put Adam into a deep sleep, took a rib from Adam's side and formed a woman out of it. Then God woke Adam up again and brought the woman to him.

I wondered what it must have been like for Adam to wake up and see Eve for the very first time, standing there in all her splendiferous glory! Wow! The smile on Adam's face must have been about a mile wide!

As I pictured the scene in my mind, I suddenly felt like God was looking down at me in the exact same way. Here I was, in the midst of God's beautiful creation, yet I was all alone. I had no one *like me* with whom I could truly share my life and help me do the work God had called me to do. But God had seen my loneliness! And He had created a woman just for me! He brought her to me in Houston, and she was sitting right there, right now—in the other room!

This was it! This was the answer I was waiting for, the answer I was hoping for! God *did* want me to marry Noël, and He had worked out everything so we could finally be together!

I hesitated only for a moment, wondering if I should pray some more or ask my friends again or somehow get another confirmation from anywhere else. But I had already sought out those answers from everyone else, and I was only waiting on God—and God had answered! I was so excited I couldn't wait another minute!

I jumped up off the floor and ran down the hall to tell Noël. I didn't stop to look in the mirror as I ran, but I'm sure if I did, the smile on my face would have been about a mile wide!

I sat down on the couch next to Noël and told her that God had given me my answer! I knew I could marry her now. Would she marry me?

"Are you sure?" she asked.

I told her everything I had read and all that God had been saying to me through it. I told her all the hopes and dreams I had for our life together and why I thought she was the one for me. I told her how very much I loved her and how very much I loved the idea of spending the rest of my life with her.

Noël then told me that she had just been reading from a devotional book called *Encourage Me*. In the book, the author said, "Read Isaiah 40:28-31. Do it right now." So Noël opened up her Bible to that passage, which happened to be her favorite passage in the whole Bible:

"Do you not know? Have you not heard? The LORD is the everlasting God, the Creator of the ends of the earth. He will not grow tired or weary, and His understanding no one can fathom. He gives strength to the weary and increases the power of the weak. Even youths grow tired and weary, and young men stumble and fall; but those who hope in the LORD will renew their strength. They will soar on wings like

eagles; they will run and not grow weary, they will walk and not be faint" (Isaiah 40:28-31).

When Noël read those words she had decided that she was going to put her full hope in the Lord for this, too, to wait on Him for as long as it took. She said she was willing to wait forever if that's how long it took for me to get my "final" answer. She had gone back to reading her devotional book again when I ran into the room—with my eyes wide open!

We were both so happy, we started to cry. I got down on one knee, held her hands in mine and asked Noël if she would marry me.

She said, "Yes!"

I didn't have a ring, but I had a Word from God, and that was worth more to me than gold and diamonds. (I did eventually give her a ring with gold and diamonds, because that still meant a lot to her!)

We hugged and kissed and talked and prayed for a long, long time. Then we spent the rest of the day at Hermann Park, a beautiful place in the middle of Houston. We walked and talked some more, looking at the animals in the nearby zoo. We rode paddle boats on the lake, and it started to rain—a soft, beautiful rain. We didn't care! We were never so happy; we were never so in love. The rain stopped and the sun came out. Everything was even more beautiful than before!

From that day on I never looked back and never once doubted that Noël was a gift from God to me. We started making plans for our upcoming wedding and set the date for April 29th, about four months away.

As much as I looked forward to my wedding day with Noël, and knew it would be special in its own way, *this* was the day God answered my prayers, the day He said He would give me the desire of my heart, to marry Noël. I wanted to shout for joy—and I did!

Chapter 20:

Gift Wrapping

In the months leading up to our wedding, Noël and I took a new approach to our physical relationship. By this time, both of us had made commitments to sexual purity before and within marriage.

I had made my commitment at a men's conference led by Ed Cole the summer before. At the end of the conference, Ed invited any of the single men in the room to stand if they wanted to make a commitment of saving the glory of their virginity for their wife at the time of their marriage. Some of my friends and I, along with many of the other single men in the room, stood up. Although I had already done more sexually by that point than I should have done, I had asked God for His forgiveness and had been given a clean slate. I wanted to keep it clean! It turned out God was willing to give us a fresh start at any time, at any moment that we were willing to take that step with Him. This was still a fairly new concept for me, but I was glad to take a stand, and by standing up I felt like I was making a bond with God to keep it.

Noël had made a commitment that summer to keeping herself sexually pure as well. As she was teaching others what God intended for dating and relationships, Noël realized that she had gone too far in her physical relationships in the past, and she had hurt herself and others in the process. She, too, wanted to save any future sexual activity for marriage.

We both knew it would be hard to do this, but we were willing to do whatever it took to safeguard the beauty of sex for marriage.

During our engagement, I met with a counselor who challenged me to consider waiting to even *kiss* Noël until our wedding day. He felt that given our past physical relationships, kissing could stir up way too many emotions that would make it even harder for us to keep our commitment to sexual purity. After a few days of thinking and praying about it, I agreed with his thoughts.

I brought the idea up to Noël of not kissing until our wedding day, but she wasn't so sure she was ready to back up that far! She loved physical touch, both for the sensations it evoked and for the emotional reassurance of my love.

But after a few failed attempts at trying to "just kiss"—some of which ended up with both of us on the floor, in compromising positions and with half our clothes on the ground next to us—Noël agreed that we'd better draw the line back at a friendly kiss on the cheek.

Needless to say, we could hardly wait for our wedding day! We were not only going to get to kiss again, but to do something neither of us had ever done before: to make love, fully and completely, as husband and wife.

On the night before our wedding, I couldn't believe the day was almost here. I wasn't nervous, but I was curious as to what full sexual intercourse would be like with Noël. I also couldn't wait to wake up next to her the day after we got married. I was getting so tired of having to say good night and then go back to my own house without her. I just wanted to stay with her forever. Only one more night alone, and from then on I could hold her and love her and kiss her and caress her all night long, and all the next morning, and all the next night, and all the next morning and every night after that—for as long as we both shall live. Hallelujah!

The photographer for our wedding warned us that sometimes he had to tell couples not to smile so much on their wedding day—not because he didn't want them to be happy—

but because they were SO happy that their smiles would look unnaturally large in the pictures! As I lay there in bed on the night before my wedding, I knew exactly what he meant. But I also knew there was no way I was going to be able to tone down my smile, whether I wanted to or not!

When I woke up the next morning, I was deliriously happy. All of the planning, preparing, praying and waiting were done. Now it was just a matter of saying our vows in front of our family and friends and driving off with a sign on the back of our car to let people know we were "JUST MARRIED!"

As I stood at the front of the church waiting for Noël to appear at the other end of the long aisle, I couldn't help but be thankful to God who had brought me so far. He had saved me, redeemed me, forgiven me and given me a new life. Now—on this glorious day—He was giving me a wife. The music played, and the bridesmaids made their way down the aisle. Then it was Noël's turn.

The music changed, the people stood up and Noël stepped into the doorway, flat-out stunning in her white silk dress, with her bare skin showing just above her breasts and a single strand of white pearls gracing her beautiful neck. Noël's face—framed by the pearls below and the open veil above—was more than stunning. It was radiant.

She walked down the aisle, and her father placed her hands in mine. Then we said our vows—mine through tears and sniffles; hers with eloquence and poise.

I went first:

"Noël, ever since I read Psalm 20 that says, 'May He give you the desire of your heart,' I've known that you are the desire of my heart. If I could ask God for only one gift in my lifetime, it would be to marry you. Today, God is answering my prayer. I promise to treat you as a gift—to love you always, to honor and respect you, to be faithful to you and to treat you with care and kindness. I promise to put Christ at the center of our marriage, to look to Him as an example of how to love you and to look to

the Bible to guide us in all things. Noël, you are beautiful. You are kind and encouraging and have an abundant love of life. I can't think of anything more fun than to spend the rest of my life with you. I promise to always love you, not based on how you act, or on my feelings, but because you are a treasure in God's eyes. Noël, I love you, and I want more than anything in the world to be your husband."

Noël followed:

"Nick, I gladly accept you as a gift from God, to be my husband. I love you and promise in the presence of our friends and relatives to obey you, trust you, encourage you and be faithful to you, forever. You make it so easy for me to love you because you know God's love for you and are able to return that love so easily. You are so gentle and patient, a truly kind and forgiving person. God has blessed you with many wonderful gifts. My greatest desire is to spend the rest of my life with you. With the help of God, I will do my best to love you unconditionally, like the love Jesus Christ has for us, and to forgive as He forgives us. I promise to look to Him for help and guidance whenever we are struggling. With the help of God, I know that our marriage will last for as long as we both shall live."

We exchanged our rings, said our "I do's," and the pastor pronounced us "husband and wife."

And the best part of the day was still to come.

After a reception at the church, where we met with guests, ate Blue Bell ice cream and shared our first dance as a married couple, we drove off to our hotel for the night—the French-themed Hotel Sofitel.

When we got to the room, Noël looked as stunning as ever. We wanted to eat some of the food from the reception which had been boxed up for us, so Noël was going to take off her dress to get comfortable. I asked if she could leave it on for just a few more minutes. She looked like a present, all wrapped up—just for me. We sat on the bed, with Noël in her beautiful white dress and me in my tuxedo, eating fresh fruit, brie cheese with raspberry jam and crackers, and champagne and chocolates for dessert.

When I was in junior high, *Life* magazine did a photo spread on the wedding of Lady Diana, who became a princess on her wedding day when she married Prince Charles. The picture from the magazine that stood out to me the most—and which I've remembered ever since—was taken just after the wedding. Diana was sitting on a chair with her little nieces and nephews, who were playing and sitting all around her. Her white silk dress billowed out, around and underneath them all. That dress—it was just so "touchable." I wished I could reach out and feel the folds and puffs and poufs for myself. It was like a scene from the perfect fairy-tale wedding.

Now, sitting before me was my very own princess. As Noël said on the day I asked her to marry me, this was better than any fairy tale, because this was real—and it was happening to us!

After finishing our brie and jam and drinking a few sips of champagne, the time had come—the time that would unite us as husband and wife, in a way that was more fun than any wedding ceremony at a church full of people and more binding than any piece of paper signed by a pastor, two witnesses and the county clerk.

This—making love for the very first time with the woman who had become the desire of my heart—*this* was what marriage was all about, when "the two shall become one flesh," as described by God in the Bible, and reiterated by Jesus, His Son.

With love and excitement, curiosity and anticipation, desire and arousal and mutual affection, Noël invited me to take off her dress—to unwrap the gift that both she and God were so happy to give me.

As I unbuttoned each of the twenty small buttons down the back of her dress, Noël helped me to take off my jacket, my tie, my shirt and my socks. Layer by layer we unwrapped each other like no birthday or Christmas present we had ever unwrapped.

Then there we were: naked and unashamed, fully in love and full of delight. We kissed, we touched and we began to make love—a deep and penetrating love that neither of us had ever experienced before.

It felt... *wonderful.*

There was nothing in my life that compared to it—kissing her lips, touching her breasts, looking into her eyes and noticing every smile, every movement, every sensation. Noël invited me in, pulled me in and pressed her body as close to mine as she could until neither of us could hold back any longer. With a flush of heat and a passionate tongue-entwined kiss, we exploded with pleasure that went beyond any meter on any conceivable scale of delight.

We felt like the couple at the end of the movie *The Princess Bride* when they finally got together and kissed. With the sun setting in the background, the narrator said:

"Since the invention of the kiss, there have only been five kisses that were rated the most passionate, the most pure. This one left them all behind."

We continued kissing and caressing and holding each other tight, taking long, deep breaths to get some air back into our lungs.

Then we laid there next to each other—both thoroughly and completely satisfied—touching, kissing, smiling, laughing, gazing and amazing. We thanked God, and each other, for the incredible gifts we had just unwrapped.

We couldn't wait to do it again... and again... and again... for the rest of our lives. And we did.

PART 5 ~ HOLDING ON

Chapter 21:
Perfect Ten

Let me catch my breath for a minute before going on. Most love stories and fairy tales end about here. The music swells, "The End" appears and the credits roll.

But that's just when all the *good stuff* starts to happen! Everything else up to that point—all the hard work and effort, the passion and pain, the false starts and restarts—is just the prelude to the main theme, the appetizer to the feast, the battle before the victory when the couple finally gets to get on with their lives and live "happily ever after."

Our wedding day was great, but it wasn't the *best* day of our lives (that would imply it was downhill from there on out!). Our wedding day was just the *first* day of the *best days* of our lives.

The next day, Noël and I woke up next to each other for the very first time as husband and wife. We spent the rest of the day relaxing in the glow of all that God had done for us up to that point.

We couldn't stop smiling all through the day, starting with more intimate kisses in bed, followed by breakfast in bed, followed by still more intimate kisses in bed. Then we went out for a swim at the hotel pool, where the sunny day highlighted the sunny glow emanating from my wife (I loved the sound of that: *my wife!*). We swam and held each other close, letting the warm water from the waterfall in the pool run over our heads as we kissed and talked and touched some more. Noël's eyes, her face, the skin on her shoulders (and everywhere else) were magnetic, drawing me close to her, continually.

We ended the day with dinner at *Chez Colette,* the hotel's exquisite French restaurant, then retreated to our room for another delightful night. The next day, we drove to the airport nearby where we took a flight to Las Hadas, a resort in Mexico on the coast of the Pacific Ocean.

Las Hadas was the same resort where they filmed the movie *10.* I was too young to watch *10* when the movie came out (and I'm probably too old to watch it now!), but I do remember seeing the previews, with Bo Derek in her braided cornrows, walking along the beach in slow motion. If Bo Derek was a 10, Noël was an 11!

Noël was beautiful from head to toe and from fingertip to fingertip. I loved every part of her: her hair, her eyes, her nose, her cheeks, her ears, her lips, her eyebrows, her shoulders, her chest, her breasts, her nipples, her stomach, her back, her bottom, her arms, her legs and her most intimate areas.

But perhaps what attracted me to her so much—and her to me—was the fact that now we *belonged* to each other. As the Bible says:

"The wife's body does not belong to her alone but also to her husband. In the same way, the husband's body does not belong to him alone but also to his wife" (1 Corinthians 7:4).

There was something about being in that exclusive, committed relationship that added all the more to our mutual attraction. Noël was mine and I was hers; we *belonged* to each other.

I felt like a friend of mine who had received a bouquet of flowers one day for a special event. Her family had received several bouquets of flowers, each addressed to the whole family. But this one bouquet was addressed specifically to her. It wasn't necessarily the most colorful or the prettiest or the fanciest bouquet the family had received; in fact, it was quite plain and simple. Yet because this particular bouquet was addressed *to her,* this was the bouquet she treasured the most.

Sometimes I wondered if my over-the-top attraction for Noël was for a similar reason. She had a natural beauty, no doubt, but never in a "glamor shot" kind of way. She wore little makeup and little jewelry and was most comfortable in jeans and a T-shirt, which was her usual attire (except at night, when she wore only a T-shirt—much to my delight!).

But like my friend's favorite bouquet was the one that was addressed specifically to her, perhaps the reason I was so attracted to Noël was because God had addressed her specifically to me. In fact, I was rarely attracted to anyone *except* Noël. I felt that God had somehow put in my heart a singular love just for her.

I wondered if my love for Noël was like the love the prince felt in the Rodgers and Hammerstein musical, *Cinderella.* When the prince first met Cinderella, he sang:

"Do I love you because you're beautiful,
Or are you beautiful because I love you?
Am I making believe I see in you
A girl too lovely to be really true?
Do I want you because you're wonderful,
Or are you wonderful because I want you?
Are you the sweet invention of a lover's dream,
Or are you really as beautiful as you seem?"

Did I love Noël because she was beautiful, or was she beautiful because I loved her? Did I want her because she was wonderful, or was she wonderful because I wanted her? Was she the sweet invention of my dreams, or was she really as beautiful as she seemed?

To be honest, I didn't know and I didn't care! All I knew was that I loved her deeply and thought she was the most beautiful woman in the world—a perfect "10."

At this point in the story, a good storyteller would talk about something disastrous that happened next—but it didn't!

When we got home from our honeymoon, our new life

together went from great to greater, and our first year together set the tone for the rest of our years to come.

One of the books I read prior to marriage that helped set the tone for our sex life in particular was called *Intended for Pleasure*, written by a medical doctor and his wife, Dr. Ed and Gaye Wheat.

Although I had been sexually active before marriage, I had never made love fully with anyone before my wedding day and I wanted to make sure I knew what I was doing! The Wheat's book helped me to do just that. Plus, I learned several things that influenced my view of sex and our enjoyment of it.

For instance, I learned that human beings are the only creatures on the planet who can make love face-to-face. I had no idea! While some couples go to great lengths to find unusual positions to make love, one of the most unusual in the whole world is the one that is most natural for a man and a woman—to look deeply into each other's eyes while making love. This design is a gift from God, given only to human beings. Noël and I were always so thankful for this gift from Him, and we never tired of making love face-to-face.

Another thing I learned from the Wheat's book was that men and women take different lengths of time to become aroused and reach a climax. While men can typically go from initial arousal to climax in a matter of minutes, women, on average, take twenty minutes or more to do the same. Men, therefore, will sometimes mistake a woman's slower pace as a lack of sexual interest—when in reality their pace has been set by God. Women, on the other hand, sometimes mistake a man's quickness to be gratified as a lack of care for their spouse—when the man's pace has been set by God, too.

Knowing these differences from the outset of our marriage helped us make the most of them, rather than be frustrated by them. Noël loved being touched and stroked and massaged—and I loved touching and stroking and massaging her! Even though I might have been ready to make love fully within minutes of all this touching, she wanted to enjoy all the touching even longer. No problem! That meant more touching and stroking and massaging for me! I always found it to be a great adventure in exploration.

I would talk to her, massage her and smother her with kisses all over her body, whether I slowly massaged and kissed every finger on her hands, or stroked and kissed her most private areas: her breasts or her bottom or that most intimate place on her body. She, in turn, would talk to me and stroke me and encourage me along the way! I was thrilled with it all, and she was further aroused in the process.

I was also fully aware that it was no small thing for Noël to invite me into those private places of her body. Those private areas were off limits to everyone else in the world. And the fact that she invited only me into them satisfied both my physical longings and my emotional longings in a deep, deep way—making this one of the reasons that being joined together as husband and wife was such a delicate and precious coupling.

After an extended warm-up period like this, both of us were usually ready to make love fully. By waiting so long to do so, I was able to keep from climaxing too early, and she was much closer to climaxing by the time we *were* fully intimate. Face-to-face by God's unique design for men and women, Noël and I would consummate our love with a climactic surge of joy and pleasure. We would then hold onto each other for as long as we wanted, eventually falling asleep, whether together or apart, with a smile on each of our faces.

From the beginning of our marriage, we enjoyed extended sessions of lovemaking like this over and over and over again. God never put a restriction on how often we *could* make love— nor how often He *expected* us to make love. So we made love like this as often as we wanted!

I'd have to repeat this chapter over and over, thousands of times, to convey how much we enjoyed making love like this! While that might get tiring to read over and over, Noël and I never got tired of exploring each other's bodies in this way. And by God's miraculous and life-renewing design, nearly every time we made love seemed like the first time all over again (except, perhaps, with a little more experience).

While God didn't tell us in the Bible how often we should make love, He *did* tell us that we were not to deprive each other of these intimate moments unless both of us agreed and only for a limited time. The Bible says:

"Do not deprive each other except by mutual consent and for a time, so that you may devote yourselves to prayer. Then come together again so that Satan will not tempt you because of your lack of self-control" (1 Corinthians 7:4-5).

For Noël and me, "coming together" like this usually meant one, two or maybe three times a week; sometimes less, sometimes more.

When Noël was tired or when we didn't have as much time, she was happy for me to just massage her body with mine, letting me come to a climax without her, or she would touch me in a way to bring me to a climax on my own. Before we got married, I had committed to Noël that I wouldn't please myself sexually when I was alone, but only experience sexual release when I was with her. The counselor who suggested we not kiss until marriage also suggested this idea to me, based on my past sexual promiscuity, as a way to ensure that I always kept my focus on Noël. For us, it worked incredibly well, and several times Noël and I both credited this for helping to keep our love life alive!

Noël appreciated my focused commitment to her, and she was happy to indulge me whenever she sensed this was on my heart or mind—even if it wasn't on hers. Oftentimes, when she would try to please me in this way, and without planning to involve herself, she would get drawn into all the excitement anyway. When she did, and after reaching a mutual climax, she would often say, "Why don't we do this every day?!?!"

Suffice it to say, we both *loved* making love, whether in the most natural, unique-to-humans position, or sometimes in other, but similarly satisfying ways, whether standing up by a window on a starry night, or making love like the rest of the creation, front to back, or touching each other on a long car ride home, to keep each other awake (Kids: don't try this at home—texting while driving isn't the only thing that can cause distracted driving!) More often than not, however, we returned to making love in the way that only a man and a woman can enjoy, face-to-face, talking, kissing and caressing each other through it all.

As good as this was, I still haven't described one of the most exciting parts about making love with Noël: bearing fruit that would last.

Chapter 22:

Sexual Blessings

Before we were married, Noël told me she wanted to have twelve kids. *Twelve!* For a guy who had just come out of homosexuality, that made me laugh! Noël was the sixth out of nine, and she said she always wished there were more kids around to play with! That made me laugh again!

I was the last of three kids, and while I loved growing up with my older sister and brother, by the time they went off to college, I loved having the house to myself, too. Three kids seemed like a good amount to me.

But I loved Noël—and I loved having sex with her—so if she really wanted twelve, I was willing to give it a try!

Whether Noël and I would have, or could have, twelve kids, we didn't know. But planning for twelve from the beginning helped us to make a couple of decisions on the front end of our marriage that would impact it for good.

First, I wanted to make sure I could support our family on just my income. Noël wanted to stay home and raise our kids if we had any, so we chose a one-bedroom apartment that was close to work and which we could afford on my salary alone. We sold one of our cars to start saving money, and even though Noël and I were both making similar amounts at our full-time jobs in corporate America, we decided to live on my income alone from the start to make sure we didn't overextend ourselves. Everything we did, we did with the future in mind, enjoying the present as much as possible along the way.

Second, we decided to wait a year before having kids—as we expected the rest of our lives would be filled with them! At first, we weren't sure if this was the right approach or not. We had heard and read some good arguments for *not* using birth control, arguments which were both biblical and practical. But in the end, neither of us found these reasons compelling enough in our situation. We weren't trying to withhold anything from God that He might want from our marriage (in terms of having children), but we were looking forward to being on our own for a year, if we could, before launching into our childbearing and childrearing years. I was struck by a passage in the Bible that talked about the importance of the first year of marriage which gave me a helpful perspective.

The Bible said that even if a country was going to war, a man who was newly married was prohibited from going—so he could stay home and please his wife instead:

"If a man has recently married, he must not be sent to war or have any other duty laid on him. For one year he is to be free to stay at home and bring happiness to the wife he has married" (Deuteronomy 24:5).

Although this passage didn't talk specifically about having children, it highlighted for me the importance of giving priority to that first year of marriage and making it special. For us, that helped us make our decision to use some form of birth control during our first year. Then came the consideration of which form to use.

Noël tried taking the pill, but it made her so sick the first time that she never tried it again. We were also concerned that the pill might unintentionally kill a child who had been conceived, but which had not yet attached the lining of the womb, as the dosage of the pills was pretty strong at that time. For the same reason, we ruled out IUDs (Intrauterine Devices), which floated around the womb, continually scraping the lining of the womb, and which we feared might also unintentionally destroy a life that had conceived, not just prevent its conception. Condoms and creams seemed the easiest methods, which we decided to use initially in our marriage, but which turned out to be less than reliable for some of our friends, and less than satisfying for us!

In the end, the method which worked the best for us and which we used the longest, was the rhythm method. This method involved Noël taking her temperature every day to determine when she was most likely to be ovulating, and then not making love during her most fertile days of the month. If we *did* want to make love on those days, we used a condom and took extra care. The rhythm method worked best for us all around, freeing us up to make love, most of the time at least, without even a thin sheath of rubber between us—making the experience much more enjoyable, too. Nothing else we ever tried ever seemed better to us than using the natural lubrication that God had designed each of our bodies produce, which made our lovemaking smooth and fun.

At the end of our first year of marriage, we felt we were ready for kids (if it's ever possible to *really* be ready for kids!) and, if we did have them, we would be thrilled. This also freed us from any restrictions in our lovemaking, at any time of the month, which was astounding! Making love with Noël—with the thought that she might get pregnant from our lovemaking —somehow made sex with her even more amazing.

Within a few weeks of our decision to be open to having kids, Noël was pregnant—and we were both thrilled. (We also discovered that during pregnancy, Noël's hormones doubled daily, making her more eager than ever to make love! Could life get any better!?!?)

Those months of making love during pregnancy were some of the best of our lives. Noël felt more pleasure, in part because of her increased hormones. She also looked even more radiant to me, if that were possible, because she fairly glowed while pregnant. And the mere thought of Noël being pregnant, knowing that it was a result of our intimacy, aroused me all the more during our subsequent times together! If for no other reason than the heightened experience we had during sex, pregnancy was *very, very good* to both of us.

Then our daughter was born! I couldn't believe how much I loved this little girl—this little creation of God.

My amazement at sex went through the roof. How could God use something as fun as sex to create something as complicated as a child? Noël and I really had "become one flesh," not only by the joining of our bodies together while making love, but now in this little 6 pound, 11 ounce girl who was clearly part of Noël and part of me. We named her Grace.

A few days after Grace was born, I was talking to a group of elderly residents at a nursing home about her. I could hardly contain my joy when trying to describe how much I loved her, spreading my arms out as far as possible on each side to try to show the extent of my love. Even though all Grace could do was eat, sleep and make messes Noël and I had to clean up, we loved her deeply.

How much, then, must God love each one of us, I wondered, *even when sometimes all we can do is eat, sleep and make messes He has to clean up?* Somehow, having this little baby girl helped me understand God's love for me in a way I'm not sure I could *ever* have understood without having her. Even before Grace was born, when she was just growing in Noël's womb, my perspective on kids was already changing.

From the day we found out Noël was pregnant, I became more thrilled, more nervous and more curious about this whole idea of bringing a child into the world. As Grace grew in Noël's womb, we were able to see her grow, feel her move and talk to her and pray over her. She was real, she was coming and we couldn't wait to see her face-to-face (we didn't actually know she was a "she" until we finally saw her in the flesh).

Like the grinch whose heart had grown two sizes one day, I felt like my heart had grown two sizes, too, as our little baby grew within Noël.

I realized that prior to Noël's pregnancy, I had been pursuing love and sexual intimacy in ways that really "missed the forest for the trees." I was pursuing sex for my own sake, my own desires, my own pleasure, my own feelings of self-worth and self-satisfaction, hardly realizing that God had created sex for reasons that went way beyond my own. God created sex for intimacy *and* fruitfulness, but I had been using sex in ways that sometimes destroyed intimacy and would never be fruitful, no matter how I matched the parts. As always, God's ways and thoughts were much higher than mine. As the Bible says:

"As the heavens are higher than the earth, so are My ways higher than your ways and My thoughts than your thoughts" (Isaiah 55:9).

After Grace was born, Noël quit her job at the office and started her new job at home, raising our children.

Interestingly, a couple of changes took place in Noël's body after giving birth. The first one really scared us!

We weren't sure what was wrong, but sex was just plain, painful for Noël—when it had been so terrific before the birth. We were afraid something may have gone wrong during delivery, even though Grace was born by C-section because she would have been born breech otherwise. We wondered what had changed?

We set up an appointment with Noël's doctor and asked him what might be wrong. He just laughed and suggested we get some KY Jelly, an artificial lubricant, and said Noël would be just fine again.

Hesitant and unsure if the doctor *really* understood the pain Noël was describing, we did as he suggested. Like magic, it turned out that the doctor was right! Noël's hormones had dropped dramatically after giving birth, plus her body no longer produced the same amount of natural lubrication it had before. The doctor gave us such a simple fix that we would have missed had we not gone to ask him. Noël was relieved, and so was I, as she was beginning to fear the worst: spending the rest of her life in pain every time she tried to make love, rather than enjoying one of the greatest pleasures God had given her.

The other change in Noël's body was that she no longer had a period—and wouldn't likely have one as long as she was nursing Grace regularly and exclusively. In God's design, nursing this way provides a natural spacing for children which we hadn't known about before. Noël's period didn't return until Grace started taking other food and liquids in addition to nursing. When that happened, Noël's period returned, and soon we were expecting again. But that nine-month hiatus due to Noël's consistent nursing was a welcome break for all of us as we adjusted to our new life together.

Eighteen months later, Noël gave birth again, to a boy we nicknamed Dune, short for Dunamis, the Greek word from which we get the English word "dynamite." (In the Bible, the word *dunamis* means "the power of God to cause a miracle to happen," and Dune's birth was miraculous to us, as the doctor thought at one point that Dune had died in Noël's womb. After crying and praying that night, we were crying and rejoicing the next day when we saw his tiny heartbeat on an internal ultrasound monitor! It was truly a miracle!)

After giving birth to Dune, Noël nursed him even longer and her period didn't return until almost a year and a half later. When her period returned, Noël was soon pregnant again. Nine months after that, she gave birth to our third baby, a daughter. We named her Blessing.

While the Bible calls children blessings from God (such as "Blessed is the man whose quiver is full of them," from Psalm 127:5a), it wasn't until Noël was pregnant with our third child that I really, truly *felt* blessed by God. I had been so excited, but so nervous, before the birth of our first child, and so excited, but so worried about the health of our second. But from the moment I suspected Noël was pregnant with our third, I thought, "Wow! I really am blessed by God!"

Just as people would feel blessed if they were given two or three cars or two or three houses, I felt blessed to be given two or three children. Of course, two or three children—just like two or three cars or two or three houses—meant two or three times the amount of work, as anyone who has two or three (or more) of any of those things will agree!

But first and foremost, I had finally discovered that the blessing of sex with Noël went beyond just the wonderful intimacy we shared. The blessing of sex also included the blessing of children from God—and we were happy to receive them from His hand.

Chapter 23:

Baby Valor

Six years into our marriage, and three children later, Noël and I had a good start going on those twelve children she wanted to have. By that time, we had moved back to Illinois to be closer to our families. I had quit my computer job at the oil company to go into full-time ministry, creating and running a website to encourage others in their faith.

A church in Dallas, Texas, heard about us and our walk of faith, and the pastor called me to see if I would be interested in working with their church. I wasn't quite ready to move our growing family back to Texas, as it felt like we had just moved from Texas a few years earlier and had bought a cute, little two-bedroom house in Illinois—complete with a white picket fence, a hundred live rose bushes and a thirty-foot, in-ground swimming pool in the backyard. We loved our new house and our new life back in Illinois, but I told the church I'd come and work with them for a month and see what God might do.

A few weeks before I left for Dallas, Noël found out she was expecting again. Since it was still early in her pregnancy, and Noël had good help from family and friends in the area, I went ahead with my planned trip.

Day after day in Dallas, I saw miracles happen in the lives of the people coming to the church: those who had struggled for years with addictions were set free, marriages that had been on the rocks were restored and couples who couldn't have children conceived. It was incredible!

But near the very end of my stay there, Noël called, distressed. She was bleeding, and the doctors were afraid she might be having a miscarriage. I changed my flight immediately and got on the next plane to St. Louis, where our pastor in Illinois picked me up and drove me four hours back to our house. As I rushed into the front door, Noël and a friend greeted me, but they were crying. It turned out that half an hour earlier Noël had miscarried our little baby.

Noël walked me back to the bathroom to see the baby, which she had miscarried in the tub and had set on the counter just before coming to greet me at the door. She picked up the baby and handed it to me—the tiniest baby I had ever seen, only six weeks old since conception.

I was amazed as I held its tiny, little body, hardly taking up any space at all in the palm of my hand. Yet it was a complete baby, with tiny, little arms and tiny, little legs. I spread out its tiny, little, feather-like fingers, and looked into its tiny, little, dark eyes.

We had already picked out a name for this baby: Valor, meaning strong and courageous. Now I looked down at our little baby Valor. Strong. Courageous. Yet so very tiny—so very fragile. I couldn't help but cry.

We went to the hospital, where the doctor performed a D&C, a procedure to clear out any remaining tissue from Noël's womb since her bleeding still wouldn't stop. We returned home in the middle of the night, with the loss and grief and pain from the day weighing heavy on our hearts. There was nothing we could do to change what had happened.

As I went to bed that night, I couldn't help but picture our little baby Valor that I had held in my hand that afternoon. As much as I hated losing our baby, God had given me a unique gift as a result: a chance to see what He saw whenever He lost one of His own precious little children. I couldn't help but think of some of my friends who had lost their children to miscarriage—or to abortion—and the loss and grief and pain they often felt when they realized there was nothing they could do to change what had happened.

It would be several years later until I learned how I might offer them some help and healing, when I had a chance to meet Norma McCorvey, also known as "Jane Roe" in the famous Supreme Court case *Roe vs. Wade.*

Norma was speaking at an event fifteen minutes from my hometown regarding the landmark case which made her assumed name, Jane Roe, famous—and which made abortion legal for the first time in all fifty states of the United States. I thought it would be interesting to hear what she had to say, but I was *stunned* to find out that she had never actually had an abortion. She gave birth to her daughter and gave her up for adoption before the case made its way to the Supreme Court. I was even *more stunned* to find out how thankful she was that she didn't have an abortion. I had assumed, wrongly, that she would have been pleased to have won her case at the Supreme Court.

After winning the case, Norma went to work at an abortion clinic herself. Ironically, but not accidentally, a national right-to-life group moved its headquarters next door to that clinic. While Norma was initially appalled that the group had moved in next door, she eventually warmed up to a seven-year old daughter of one of the group's members—a little girl who was about the age of the girl Norma had given up for adoption. Every day, this little girl gave "Miss Norma" a hug as Norma came into the building. Norma was won over by the love of this little girl, who invited Norma to church where Norma happily gave her life to Christ.

When Norma had first gone to the lawyers who took her case to the Supreme Court, they told her that the fetus in her womb was just a "piece of tissue." In Norma's own words, she says that the final turning point for her eventual change of heart towards abortion came while looking at a fetal development poster that showed babies at various stages of life inside the womb. Norma said:

"Yet something in that poster made me lose my breath. I kept seeing the picture of that tiny, ten-week-old embryo, and I said to myself, that's a baby! It's as if blinders just fell off my eyes and I suddenly understood the truth—that's a baby!"

Norma had seen a picture of what God had let me hold in my hands: one of his precious creations, only weeks old after conception. The impact of that image on Norma's life was as profound as the impact of holding baby Valor had on mine. What a gift, life! And what a loss when it is gone, for whatever reason, at any stage.

As a friend of mine said, after losing one of her teenage friends, "I hate death. I don't think I'll *ever* get used to it."

And God doesn't want us to.

Thankfully, Norma found forgiveness in Christ for the things she had done in her life which she regretted (just like I had received forgiveness for the things I had done in my life and regretted). Norma said:

"I still feel very badly. I guess I always will. But I know I've been forgiven."

I was still so stunned when I heard Norma's message that I met with her afterwards to talk. Although I learned that her story was true and was well-documented, somehow I had never heard it before. *Was she really saying that she wished Roe vs. Wade was overturned?* I thought. So I asked her if what I thought she was saying was true.

"Yes," she said, "that's true."

I asked her if she would mind writing it down for me on a piece of paper. She said she'd be glad to, took a piece of paper and wrote:

"I wish R v. W was overturned. Ms. Norma McCorvey."

Wow, I thought, shaking my head. I just couldn't believe it. If Norma McCorvey could feel the loss and grief and pain of a little baby's death—and I could feel the loss and grief and pain of a little baby's death—I knew others could feel it, too. And if Norma McCorvey could find forgiveness and healing by putting her faith in Christ—and I could find forgiveness and healing by putting my faith in Christ—I knew others could find forgiveness and healing, too.

As hard as it was to lose baby Valor, I was thankful God had used it to let me see one of His tiniest creations up close and personal, with my very own eyes.

Unfortunately, our little baby Valor was the first of *four* miscarriages we had that year. (We gave names to each of them: Angel, Philip, who Noël miscarried while we were on a missions trip in the Philippines, and one so tiny we named endearingly Baby-Baby.) With each loss, our grief was compounded, as the weight of each miscarriage was added to the weight of the previous ones. We seriously wondered if we would ever be able to have children again.

In the midst of that year, we had decided to move to Dallas to work with the church there, as we had seen God do so much during the month I had visited.

Ironically, we had a chance to pray with several couples who weren't able to have children—and they conceived! In spite of our own miscarriages, we could see God was doing miracles in other people's lives.

One night, a few months after Noël's fourth miscarriage, she was listening to a worship CD by a man named Don Moen. Before one of the songs, Don told the story from the Bible about a woman who came to Jesus who had been subject to bleeding for twelve years. She had been to many doctors and had used up all her money, yet she wasn't healed; she kept getting worse instead.

Then she came to Jesus, surrounded by a crowd of people, thinking, "If I just touch His clothes I will be healed." She reached out and touched the hem of His robe, and immediately she felt in her body that she had been healed. The blood stopped flowing.

Jesus, sensing that power had flowed out of Him, asked, "Who touched me?" Trembling, the woman fell at His feet and told Him what had happened. Jesus said, "Daughter, your faith has healed you. Go in peace and be freed from your suffering."

Don Moen said he didn't understand how healing worked, but he knew that if Jesus walked into the room where he was standing right then, that he could reach out to Jesus and trust that He would do whatever was best for him. Don reminded everyone that Jesus was still alive and among us, even now, and would do what was best for us, too.

As Noël listened to that CD that night, she came to the point where she relinquished all control of her situation to God. There was nothing more she could do, but she knew she could trust Jesus to do whatever was best. Noël felt God's peace pour out upon her. She felt different from that night on, and she looked different, too!

She was truly surprised then, when a few weeks later, she found out she was pregnant again. But this time she felt things were different—and this time the pregnancy held.

Nine months later, Noël gave birth to another son, Noble. Two years after that, she gave birth to yet another son, Honor, and three years after that gave birth to a daughter, Glory.

After the birth of our first three children, then the loss of the next four, God had given us three more as He continued working miracles right before our eyes.

Chapter 24:

Divine Encounters

After I married Noël, I began feeling more comfortable talking publicly about my struggles with homosexuality. I had talked about them privately with others since the day I first put my faith in Christ, but talking about them publicly was new for me.

One of the first talks I gave was to the Berean Class, the singles class where I had first come to Christ.

The singles pastor asked if I would be willing to share a longer version of my testimony with the class one Sunday morning, which by that time was running at about 200 people. The pastor thought my story would encourage them to put their trust in Christ for *any* issue they might be facing in their lives, not just homosexuality. I agreed.

After sharing my story, several people came up to tell me about their own struggles with homosexuality, or about how the message encouraged them to face the various situations they were facing.

One woman came up and said, "Oh, Nick, there's a conference for people who have struggled with homosexuality. You should go!"

"Uh, thanks," I said. But in my head, I thought, *No way! I'm not going to a conference where everyone there has struggled with homosexuality!* That was the last place I wanted to go!

Two years later, however, I found myself at that very conference! I had actually been invited to speak at another conference that same week in Washington, DC, for work, to talk about emerging computer technologies and the impact they would have on our lives. Al Gore, a senator at the time— and who would later become the vice president of the United States—was also scheduled to speak. While I was glad to be selected to speak, and had already accepted the invitation, a friend of mine asked if I would go with him to the conference on homosexuality instead. Sensing God wanted me to go with my friend, I canceled my speaking engagement at the technology conference.

As I walked up to the buildings where the conference on homosexuality was to be held, I thought, *What am I doing here? Everyone's going to know why I'm here!* And when I found out there were about 1,000 attendees signed up, I wanted to turn around and run! I had never felt so exposed. But I had come with my friend, and it was too late to turn back now.

As I began listening to the speakers, I found myself relating to so much of what they were talking about. Their thoughts, their feelings and their desires were so much like mine had been (and somewhat like they still were, but without the power that they once held over my life). Prior to coming out of homosexuality, I had never met nor heard of anyone else who had done the same. All of my friends who had been in that lifestyle were still in it. Now, here I was, surrounded by almost 1,000 people who felt what I had felt and who were in various stages of coming out of it themselves! It was, in a word, amazing!

One afternoon, I was standing on the front steps of a building, listening to a speaker who had moved his class outside as the weather was so nice. As I stood and listened at the back of the group, a man walked up to me and said, "Hi. Can you tell me what's happening here?"

I explained to him what the speaker was saying and I asked him what had brought him here.

"I'm a reporter," he said. And I panicked—big time!

A reporter! Oh, great! Now he's going to ask me some questions and put my name and picture on the front page of some newspaper, telling the world that I was gay! At least, I could tell him I *was* gay, but was now happily married to a woman. Still, the thought of it all sent a chill of fear down my spine.

He asked why I was there, so I decided to go ahead and tell him my story. *Perhaps,* I thought, *if I tell him enough about Jesus and about what He has done for me, then he'll print that, too.* If God could use my embarrassing story for His purposes, at least that would make it worth it. So I proceeded to tell him my story, pairing everything I said with a verse from the Bible. My hope was that if he was going to quote me, at least maybe he'd quote some Scripture, too. We talked for at least an hour, maybe two, walking and talking all around campus. I felt like I must have shared at least half the Bible with him that day!

When we finished talking, I invited him to a chapel service that night on campus. A woman was speaking that week and I thought he might like to hear what she had to say, plus the worship music was great. He thanked me for the conversation and we parted ways.

It turned out that he *did* come back to the chapel service that night—and put his faith in Christ. As he told me later, he *was* a reporter, but he wasn't there to cover the conference. He was there because he, too, had struggled with homosexuality. He had seen several doctors and psychologists, none of which had helped. He was plagued by his feelings of homosexuality and didn't know where else to turn. This conference was his last-ditch effort to try to find some hope.

He finally found it that day, in Jesus. He eventually quit his job as a reporter and went into full-time ministry, helping others encounter Jesus, too.

Experiences like this encouraged me to keep sharing my story with others, to the point where I finally posted my testimony on the budding Internet for all the world to see—or at least the thirty million or so who were on it at the time, as the Internet was, for the first time, available for use by the general public (thanks in large part, actually, to the efforts of then-senator Al Gore, who spoke about the idea at the technology conference which I had skipped!).

After nervously posting my testimony on the Internet, I soon heard from people in places like Athens, Greece, Cairo, Egypt and Seattle, Washington, all asking if I could pray with them. Some of the people were struggling with homosexuality, but others weren't. Many simply found my story engaging and inspiring, giving them faith to believe that God could do anything, absolutely anything, and causing them to want to put their faith in Him, too.

One day I got an email from a pastor in Europe. He had read my story and composed a long note to me, but was afraid to push the "send" button on his email. He said he had never shared what he wanted to share with me with anyone else before.

It turned out that when he and his wife got married, they tried to make love on their honeymoon and things didn't go so well—at all. They never tried again, and they never talked about it again, either. He was struggling with homosexual feelings, but was afraid to tell his wife about them.

He sent me pictures of himself and his wife. He was handsome and she was beautiful—a great looking couple—but he had so much fear of what she might think, and what the members of his church might think and what the leaders of his denomination might think, that he had never told anyone what he was feeling.

My heart went out to him, so I sent a note back saying I was so proud of him for sharing his thoughts and feelings with me. He wrote back and said, "Proud of me? That's the last thing I ever expected *anyone* to say me after sharing something like that!"

We wrote back and forth several times and he finally told

his wife about his struggles. I had encouraged him to do so after what he had told me about his wife. I thought that she—like Noël—could be one of his biggest allies in helping him through his struggle, if she only knew. When he confessed his struggle to her, it was hard for her to hear at first. But then she was amazingly relieved, having wondered all this time what *she* might have been doing wrong in their relationship. Did he not love her? Did he not think she was pretty? So many thoughts had gone through her mind. She took a long walk and came back to the house, telling him that she loved him still and wanted to do whatever she could do to help.

My new friend was undone by her response—in the best possible way. He told me that his wife had told him she loved him over and over in the past, but this was the first time he actually *believed* her. She knew everything about him now, and she still loved him! *She must really mean it!* he thought.

Of course she did, but he was now hearing it in a whole new way. They began to talk through their situation, reading up on it and getting counseling from others. Noël and I met with them in Europe on more than one occasion when we were traveling nearby, and they visited us here in the States as well. It took some time, several years in fact, for them to grow together in their physical intimacy. But they did. And in time, they gave birth to a beautiful little girl. They were thrilled for how God had helped them match their genuine love for each other with a physical love for each other that both of them had wanted so very much. And I was thankful again that I had overcome my fears enough to post my story on the Internet for others like this couple so see.

My story also seemed to continue helping people who had never struggled with homosexuality, but who were struggling with other issues in their lives. One day, I got a call from a friend telling me about a man who had just divorced his wife after twenty-four years of marriage. Their situation didn't involve homosexuality, but the man had been unfaithful to his wife by having an open affair with another woman. I knew the man, but only from a distance as he lived several states away. When I heard the news, I couldn't believe it was true. This man had grown up in a Christian home, his parents were missionaries in another country and he had come to the States with nothing and had built up a successful and thriving business in spite of it. Suddenly, everything in his life was falling apart.

After praying with Noël about his situation for a few months, I gave him a call and flew out to meet him in the Rocky Mountains. I told him of my surprise about his divorce. He said things just didn't work out.

As we sat in his car before I left, I told him the story of how God had worked in my life. He listened intently, and at the end of our conversation, his eyes watered up a bit, but not enough to form even one teardrop. I left my Bible with him, since he said he didn't have one with him at his new place, and I flew back to Illinois. I told Noël I didn't know why I even flew out there; it didn't seem to have made any difference at all.

I called him back about a month later, nervously, because he was a pretty imposing man. I wondered if I had pushed him too far with my previous conversation. But there was a men's conference coming to his city, and I said I'd go with him if he wanted to go.

He said, "Nick, you won't believe what's happened since you came out here! That night when you told me your story, you asked me if there was anything I wanted from God. I said, 'God, if there's anything, I want to get to know you. If You're really there, and You're the God of the universe, then I want to get to know you.' After you left, I sat in the car for a long, long time. I gave my life to Christ that night."

He went on to tell me that when we prayed together in the car, that was the first time *in his life* that he had ever cried. And since that night, he had cried buckets full of tears! What I thought was hardly a glint in his eye, turned out to be a tsunami in the making! He started reading the Bible I gave him, then bought one of his own, then started buying Bibles for everyone he knew! He fell in love with God that year as he got to know God better than he had ever known God in his life. Although it took him a while—and a few more hard conversations and letters between us—he eventually broke things off with his mistress, returned to his wife and fell in love with her all over again. They remarried each other and he started taking classes at a nearby seminary. He went on to become the pastor of a congregation of men and women in his city who had come to the U.S. from the same country where his parents had been missionaries! God had not only answered our prayers for him, but had added our prayers to the many, many prayers his parents and others had been praying for him for years!

I wish I could say every story has worked as well as these. They haven't. Although God can do anything, absolutely anything, God's Holy Spirit is a gentleman. He seldom comes where He's not invited.

But in conversation after conversation, where people *have* invited God's Holy Spirit to come and help them do what they can't seem to do on their own, I've seen turnarounds galore.

As one man said to another on a show called *When Calls The Heart:*

"You're a self-made man, Mr. Coulter, and you should be proud of that. But no one does it alone. We all need help at times."

We *do* all need help at times. And when that help comes from God, anything's possible—absolutely anything!

Chapter 25:

Smoke Offering

Now that we were up to six of those twelve kids that Noël had wanted, no one was more surprised than me when I felt God speaking to my heart again—this time telling me we were done having kids.

Done? I thought. *How could we be done?*

By this point I was totally loving having kids and I was looking forward to having more! But God was clear, and He spoke the same thing to me three times, on three separate occasions, each time when Noël and I were about to make love. I felt like God was not only *telling* me we were done, but He wanted me to take *extra care* to make sure Noël didn't become pregnant.

At first I didn't know why He didn't want her to get pregnant. Was something wrong? Was something terrible going to happen? Or did He know our limits and knew we had reached them? Or was there some other reason I couldn't possibly foresee? I didn't know. All I knew was that, by the third time God spoke the same thing to my heart, I needed to take it seriously.

Noël had already relinquished control over how many kids she would have after her fourth miscarriage. I was still hoping to help her fulfill that dream in her heart and keep having more if we could, but I knew it was time for me to relinquish even that desire to God, too.

From the day God called me into full-time ministry, God had been speaking to my heart in a way that I can only describe as the Bible describes in the book of Isaiah:

"Whether you turn to the right or to the left, your ears will hear a voice behind you, saying, 'This is the way; walk in it'" (Isaiah 30:21).

God was speaking to me in that way again, and while I didn't understand why, I knew I could trust Him. He had proved Himself trustworthy over and over in this way before.

I had learned that trusting God with how many children we would have didn't just mean having as many as we could have. It meant having as many as *He* wanted us to have and that was a different perspective altogether. And God wanted to involve us in that process very much, engaging our brains as well as engaging our bodies. As I was praying more about this one day, I read this passage that helped me understand it:

"Yet to all who received Him, to those who believed in His name, He gave the right to become children of God, children born not of natural descent, nor of human decision or a husband's will, but born of God" (John 1:12-13).

While this passage was talking about how to become *spiritual* children of God—by believing in Christ—it also talked about children who were born naturally, born of human decision or a husband's will. It sounded like God really did want us to use our brains as well as our bodies in determining when and how many children we would bring into the world. I knew I needed to take what He said to me very seriously.

Noël wondered if I should have a vasectomy, but I wasn't quite ready to make things that permanent yet (although even a vasectomy can sometimes be reversed, whether through surgery, or on occasion, naturally). I always liked to allow plenty of time, whenever possible, for God to correct me when I might be hearing from Him wrongly. In the meantime, we took extra care using the methods of birth control that had worked so well for us for so many years—the rhythm method when possible, and condoms when not.

Not long afterward, Noël's father had some health problems and needed some extra help, so he moved in with us.

In addition to taking care of me and the six kids, Noël now was taking care of her father, too, which some days seemed like another full-time job of its own. Noël felt more and more that I must have really heard from God. She didn't know how she could add another baby into the mix! And a few years later, Noël's mother moved in with us and we began taking care of her, too.

Eight years after God had spoken to me about not getting Noël pregnant, and taking extra care all the time whenever we made love, we both felt it was time to bring our childbearing years to a close.

With Noël's encouragement, I called a doctor in May to schedule a vasectomy. Noël was ready to make love anytime, with no inhibitions—and so was I!

Noël came with me to the doctor's appointment and sat in the waiting room while the doctor performed the procedure. I didn't know beforehand, but at the very end of the procedure, the doctor used a cauterizing tool to seal off the cuts he had made in my vas deferens, the two tubes through which sperm normally traversed. When the doctor touched the tip of the hot tool to each tube (thankfully he had applied a local anesthetic beforehand!) a thin wisp of smoke twirled up into the air as he touched each one, sealing them off permanently. To me, it looked like incense burning, perhaps like the smoke offerings made to God on His altar in ancient times. I felt like this was, in a way, *my* smoke offering to God, having offered my body to Him for His use as well as my own ever since putting my faith in Him. In some supernatural way, God had changed my life all those years ago, and I was nothing but thankful that He had. And as I looked at the thin wisps of smoke twirling up into the air, I couldn't help but think that He was thankful, too.

The nurse brought Noël back into my room, and we thanked God together, looking forward to November when we would get the six-month, "all-clear" from the doctor saying we could make love anytime, with no inhibitions.

We were also looking forward to celebrating our twenty-third Christmas together.

We had no idea it would be our last.

PART 6 ~
LETTING GO

Chapter 26:

Perfect Breasts

One (or I guess, two) of my favorite parts of Noël's body were her breasts. They were perfectly sized for her and perfectly enchanting for me.

As a pre-pubescent boy, I could never see why my pubescent friends found women's breasts to be so attractive; there was nothing alluring to me whatsoever about breasts. Even as I entered puberty and my hormones started kicking in, I still saw no difference between looking at a woman's breasts and looking at her elbows or her kneecaps. Why, I wondered, couldn't the girls in P.E. divide up into teams as "shirts" and "skins" like the guys did? Aside from what I thought was simply cultural conditioning about what men and women could and couldn't wear, I honestly didn't get it.

It was only when I had been sexually intimate with Noël for a while that I finally got it! I discovered that there was a built-in connection between a woman's breasts, her sexual arousal and the person who was touching them. Touching, kissing and caressing Noël's breasts had a way of directly stimulating her other sexual organs, as if they were connected by an unseen, sensual cord, which in turn stimulated my own sexual organs.

As I began to build up my own "database" of sexual experiences with Noël in my mind and heart and body, I found that simply glancing at her breasts brought a flush of arousal within my own body—knowing the ecstasy that touching them, kissing them and caressing them could produce, both in her and in me. No wonder the gym coach never let the girls in class be skins! There would have been more action on the court than any of us could have handled!

The difference in how I viewed women's breasts—before being sexually intimate with Noël and after—was so striking to me that it never ceased to amaze me the reaction I had whenever I had a chance to see her breasts; it always felt like I was seeing them for the very first time. Her breasts made me giddy, excited and oh-so-thankful.

In the movie *The Princess Bride,* Westley seemed to express what I felt whenever I saw Noël's breasts. When Westley's beloved Buttercup was about to plunge a dagger into her chest one day—thinking that Westley had died—Westley turned to her and said:

"There's a shortage of perfect breasts in this world. 'Twould be a pity to damage yours."

Noël's breasts *were* perfect. And until one December night, I never would have imagined that they were in danger of ever being damaged.

It was a Sunday night, after Noël and I had gone to a fun Christmas party with a small group from our church. We had read a chapter to the group from a Christmas story we had written, and had one of the guys from our group dress up as Santa Claus to pass out some foil-covered, chocolate coins to the kids. It was a terrific night, and getting better still, as Noël and I lay together in bed.

I put my hand on one of her breasts, as I often did when we were in bed, and proceeded to stroke and massage the rest of her naked body. As I returned my hand to massage her right breast again, I noticed a small lump in it—about the size of a pea—which I had never felt before. I moved my hand away, then came back to the same spot again, pressing and feeling again for the lump. It was still there.

Not sure what it was, and not wanting to worry Noël unnecessarily, I kept massaging her all over some more, returning from time to time to touch her right breast, and each time finding the same lump in the same place.

Ironically—or more likely, as God had sovereignly orchestrated it—we had been to a talk earlier that same afternoon given by a couple we knew who were doing missionary work in Kenya. One of their projects was to educate women in remote villages how to do self-exams for breast cancer. Noël and I listened with interest, asked a few questions and supported their work as we could.

Now here I was, later that same night, laying in bed with Noël and suddenly feeling a lump in her breast! Maybe I was imagining things because of the talk we had just heard. Or maybe I was more aware of things because of the talk.

I decided to tell Noël and see if she could feel it, too. I showed her where it was and moved her hand to the spot. She could feel it, too. *It couldn't possibly be cancerous (could it?)*. That would be too coincidental after the talk we had just heard. Yet the lump *did* feel like what our friends had described as they trained women to find them in Kenya.

Although we were surprised, Noël wasn't too terribly alarmed. She had some cysts show up on previous mammograms which turned out to be nothing to worry about. But she had never had anything *like this*, a lump which we could feel for ourselves. Since it was the middle of the night, and there was nothing more we could do about it, we talked about getting it checked out soon. Then we continued with our night of touching, massaging and lovemaking.

With the holidays coming up, and the fact that our regular doctor had recently moved out-of-state, it took us a few days to figure out what to do next, if anything. Given that Noël's previous mammograms and follow-ups turned out to be nothing, she wasn't too concerned.

But as the week went on, I was growing in my concern. What if this was no accident that we discovered this lump? What if God had helped us to find it and for some reason wanted us to get it checked out soon?

By Wednesday, I was ready to do something. Another friend happened to be at our house, along with her mother who had been through breast cancer, so I asked Noël if it would be okay if our friend could feel for the lump, too. Noël agreed, and our friend definitely felt the lump. Based on the way the lump felt, our friend and her mother encouraged us, *strongly*, to get it checked out right away.

Noël, however, still wasn't in much of a hurry, not only because of her previous false positives, but also because she had been reading some material that questioned whether the radiation from mammograms might actually be causing breast cancer, not just detecting it. In fact, Noël had stopped getting annual mammograms three years earlier because of those concerns.

The following Sunday night, Noël and I met again with our small group from church. After talking as a group for a while, the women decided to stay in the living room and talk and pray some more, while the men went to the kitchen to do the same. As I left the living room, I leaned over to Noël and asked her if she was going to share with the women what we were praying about that week. The women all looked at us, for I must have said it louder than I intended, and Noël said, "Well, I wasn't going to, but I guess I am now!"

Noël shared with them about the lump and how she wasn't sure if she should even do a mammogram or not, more fearful of the mammogram than what was probably just another cyst that would go away on its own. But the women convinced her to get it checked out. A friend of theirs had recently died, unfortunately, after discovering a similar lump. So the next week, we found a doctor and set up an appointment for a checkup.

Three weeks later, after an initial checkup, a mammogram, an ultrasound, another mammogram, another ultrasound and finally a needle biopsy, it was confirmed: Noël had breast cancer.

Both of us were in shock. Noël, because there was no history of breast cancer in her family and she was perfectly healthy in every other way. After giving birth to six kids, she was still at her ideal body weight, her blood work was perfect and she had been running three miles every few days, having run her first 5K earlier in the summer as a fund-raiser for orphans through our church.

I was in shock because I knew what a diagnosis of breast cancer could mean. My mom had been diagnosed with breast cancer when I was in high school. After removing her affected breast, and following that up with many rounds of chemo and radiation, the treatment seemed to have taken as much of a toll on my mom as the cancer. Although my mom was pronounced cancer-free after five years, the cancer eventually came back. Ten years after my mom's initial diagnosis, she was gone.

We began in earnest to research every possible treatment plan for Noël, from traditional surgery, radiation and chemo, to alternative approaches like strict diets, high doses of enzymes and coffee enemas.

After finding an oncologist and hearing her suggestions for surgery and chemo, Noël was still in the midst of trying to decide what to do when she started seeing blood in her urine and having intense pain in her lower back. While talking with still more friends after church that week, I learned that the woman who had recently died of breast cancer had also started having intense lower back pain soon after her initial diagnosis —an indicator the cancer had already spread to her bones.

What?!?! I thought again. *The cancer couldn't possibly have spread already (could it?).*

Noël went in for some more tests, and ten days after her initial diagnosis, we got another report: the cancer had already spread to her lungs, liver and spine. What the doctors initially thought was Stage 1 cancer and totally treatable was actually Stage 4 cancer—and there was nothing they could do to stop it. And with the type of cancer that Noël had, called "triple negative," her prognosis was even worse. Statistically, she had anywhere from three to five years left to live, perhaps less, perhaps more. But only one in a hundred women who had this type of cancer ever made it past ten years.

I suddenly felt like I had lost ten years of my life. Everything that I had watched my mom go through over ten years had just been compressed into a matter of weeks. And this was my wife they were talking about now.

We got the news on a Friday morning, by way of an emergency phone call from the doctor, as her office was two hours away from our house and she knew we would want the news right away. When we hung up the phone, as much as I wanted to hold myself together for Noël's sake, I couldn't. I cried. And cried. And cried.

I told Noël I might need a couple hours to pull myself back together, but a couple hours later, I was still crying uncontrollably. I was still crying at lunchtime and as the afternoon wore on, I was still crying more and more. I kept apologizing to Noël, but she understood and left me to cry as much as I needed. I cried on our bed for the rest of the evening, throughout the night and on into the following morning. I had never cried so much nor for so long in my life.

Twenty-four hours later I was spent. I had nothing left to cry and nothing else I could do but try to return to life and to Noël and to the kids as much as possible.

Although Noël was full of faith and hope, she was also full of practicality. That night, as we were laying in bed, she turned to me and said, "When I die, I want you to do my funeral. I can't think of anyone I'd rather have do it than you."

We both cried some more, held each other close, and fell asleep.

Chapter 27:

Steep Price

Although Noël's prognosis was dire, there were two bright spots at least (and we were happy to have *any* bright spots in the midst of all that was happening).

The first came when Noël's oncologist told Noël that the type of cancer she had was "triple negative," which meant that the cancer wouldn't respond to the normal hormone suppressants that might keep the cancer from returning. Noël *liked* her hormones and *didn't like* the idea of suppressing them! So when her oncologist told her the cancer was triple negative, Noël exclaimed, "Triple negative! That's good, right?!?!"

The oncologist looked at her with a puzzled expression and said, "Good? Hmmm... let me think how to respond to that." But from Noël's perspective, this was *great* news! She didn't want to take anything that would suppress her hormones!

The second bright spot came after we heard about Noël's terminal diagnosis, when the oncologist told us that we could cancel the breast surgery that they had previously scheduled for Noël. Since the cancer had already spread, there was no point in removing her breasts. Like Noël's response to the news of being "triple negative," my response to this news was just as thankful. Noël could keep her breasts! I definitely agreed with Westley again in *The Princess Bride* and said to Noël: "There's a shortage of perfect breasts in this world. 'Twould be a pity to damage yours."

Sparing Noël's hormones and breasts turned out to be one of the best side benefits, if there could be such a thing, of her terminal diagnosis. Over the next few months, we had some of the most memorable encounters of our lives, including a trip to New York City in April for our twenty-third wedding anniversary. My sister had told me, several years earlier, that she had seen the *Lion King* on Broadway and that it was, hands down, the most fantastic musical production she had ever seen in her life. I thought it would be great to see it someday for myself, but I kept waiting for the right opportunity. With Noël's diagnosis, I thought, *Why not now? Let's go to New York and see the show.* Noël thought it sounded great, too, so we bought tickets to see the show and bought tickets to get to New York.

Some friends had given me a check to take Noël out for a special dinner that weekend, so we decided to use the money on our first night in New York to eat at the famous Waldorf Astoria Hotel, where we wanted to try their also-famous Waldorf Salad and Red Velvet Cake. We bought tickets to see another Broadway show for that same night, since we wouldn't be seeing *The Lion King* until a few days later. I pictured in my mind what our first night in New York City might look like, with a nice, romantic dinner, followed by a show, followed by a night of making love in our hotel. But thanks to Noël's hormones that were spared, she had the reverse in mind! As soon as we landed in New York, took a cab downtown to our hotel and dropped our bags in the room, Noël kissed me and said, "Let's make love—right now!"

Surprised, but not about to protest such an overt invitation to having sex with her, I happily succumbed to Noël's kisses. She started to unbutton my shirt and pants before we even laid down on the bed. Twenty minutes later, with nothing but our socks still on our feet (we never bothered taking them off!), we were both, once again, completely and utterly satisfied. What a woman! How could God have blessed me with someone like Noël! Twenty-three years of making love with her and it never got old—and we still had the rest of the night ahead of us!

After a shower and shave, we headed down the block to the Waldorf Astoria where we asked for a window seat at the Bull & Bear restaurant. We felt somewhat like country bumpkins in the big city, but Noël couldn't have looked more ravishing in her black velvet top and matching skirt. We thoroughly enjoyed our Waldorf Salad, with the apples cut and stacked in a mound like little Lincoln logs, followed by a perfectly grilled filet mignon for me and a butter-sautéed filet of fish for her, topped off with a desert of Red Velvet Cake, colored red by the surprisingly tasty, real beet juice that had been stirred into the slightly-chocolatey batter. Best of all, though, was getting to look at Noël throughout the meal, with the afterglow of our afternoon of lovemaking still fresh on her cheeks.

After dinner, we took a fifteen-minute walk to Times Square, where we kissed and took selfies, just like they do on New Year's Eve, then we took our seats on the top row of the highest balcony in an old Broadway theater. The show that night was okay, but sitting next to Noël, holding her hand and stealing a few kisses between scenes—*that* was spectacular. The city was still bustling with nightlife as we walked back to our hotel after the show, where we climbed back into bed and talked and touched and kissed some more. It wasn't quite the way I had pictured it earlier in the day, but thanks to Noël's hormones and her intact, perfect breasts, it was much, much better.

It had only been two months since Noël's initial diagnosis, and even though she was still gorgeous on the outside, the cancer was taking its toll on the inside. Noël had decided to start taking chemotherapy, even though she hated the idea, because the doctor said it might keep the cancer at bay for a while, helping her to stay, as the doctor said, "as comfortable as possible for as long as possible." Yet even with the chemo, she was having more and more pain in her lower back, which was now spreading with the cancer to cause pain in the other joints of her body.

We took a beautiful walk in Central Park, with all of its whimsical statues and unique bridges spread out over the hills and grass and woodlands. But we had to walk fairly slowly to keep her pain manageable. She had gotten a short hair cut before the trip in preparation for when it would eventually fall out due to the chemo, and it was already starting to turn gray. (My hair was already turning gray without the chemo!) As we explored the trails through Central Park, we felt more like a couple in their seventies, taking a walk for their fifty-third anniversary, not couple in their forties taking a walk for their twenty-third. It was almost poetic, however, as we knew we probably would never get to see our fifty-third. It felt like God was giving us a chance to experience the romance that aging couples felt in what would likely be our shortened amount of time together.

On Sunday morning, we visited two great churches in the area, the historic Brooklyn Tabernacle and the newly formed Hillsong NYC. Both services filled us with a much-needed dose of inspiration.

Later that afternoon, we went to the Minskoff Theater and saw *The Lion King*, which was superb, just as my sister had said. We rounded out the weekend with another evening of lovemaking and a visit the next day to Battery Park, where we looked at the Statue of Liberty across the Hudson River. (I also got violently sick on our last day in New York, complete with all the vomiting and diarrhea that went along with it. In a way, I felt like I got the full New York experience, not just the fairy-tale version! I don't need to go back anytime soon.)

As spring turned to summer, Noël's pain and the effects of the chemo were taking more of a toll, but her passion and romance were still alive and well.

We normally took the kids on a camping trip every summer to a music festival they loved. But between Noël's pain and the forecasted heat (and alternative rock bands playing screamo music in the middle of the night), we sent the kids with some friends to camp and we stayed home.

With the house to ourselves, one of the projects we wanted to work on that week was to have Noël make a recording of thirty or forty of the Psalms for an upcoming devotional series we were preparing. Noël had a beautiful reading voice, and one of her earlier Scripture-reading projects had been extremely well received. This was a perfect week to record the Psalms while we had the whole house to ourselves.

A few days into the week, I looked at Noël one morning and said, "I wish you could take off all your clothes for a whole day. I could just look at your naked body all day long."

To my surprise, Noël said, "Okay!" and slipped off every piece of clothing she was wearing—and she stayed that way for the rest of the day! Having six kids, the first of which was born less than two years after we were married, meant that we rarely had the whole house to ourselves for even a few hours, let alone for a whole day. I was just wishing out loud, but Noël granted my wish! She had almost finished recording all the Psalms for our series by that point, but she still had one very long Psalm to go, Psalm 119. It's the longest Psalm in the Bible and the longest chapter in the Bible, with 176 verses.

It was going to take about twenty minutes to do the recording, so I sat on the couch behind her and was going to just watch as she recorded the Psalm. But I couldn't sit still for long. Noël was so beautiful, and I was so delighted that she would want to spend the whole day totally naked just for me, that I came up behind the chair where she was sitting and started touching her gently as she read.

Suffice it to say, I couldn't help but touch her from head to toe and back again as she was recording, to the point where, in the middle of Psalm 119, when she got to the words, "How sweet are Your words to my taste, sweeter than honey to my mouth," we were both so aroused she could no longer record. We made love right there, starting on the chair, then onto the floor, then back up to the couch. Afterward, with a smile on her face, she finished recording the rest of the Psalm. When she was done, she said, "I'll never look at Psalm 119 the same." "Neither will I, Noël," I said. "Neither will I."

I never imagined sharing that story for the rest of my life, until one day at church, when our pastor was speaking about Psalm 119. When he mentioned that he was going to be talking about Psalm 119 that day, I couldn't help but smile. Then I was floored when he said the word "delight"—which is one of the words that is used most often in Psalm 119—means "to fondle, particularly to fondle sexually."

The writer of the Psalm was saying that God's Word was, to him, as delightful as erotic sexual intimacy! I had no idea! Maybe it wasn't just Noël's nakedness and hormones that had aroused us so much! Rather than seeing our sexual escapade that day as possibly an unholy departure from God's Holy Word, I now wondered if God himself, the Creator of sex and the ultimate Author of those words, was underscoring and highlighting the very essence of what He was saying in those words!

As Noël said on that day we made love, "I'll never look at Psalm 119 the same."

Neither will I, Noël. Neither will I.

One more memory stands out in my mind from that summer together, one that highlights Noël's desires and her ability to make the most of every moment (and my head-over-heels desires for her). We had driven down to Champaign, where we first met in college, to do a little shopping and have some dinner.

On the way home, as the sun was setting and Noël was wishing we didn't have to go home quite yet—back to the house and all of the responsibilities that went along with it—

we saw a state park coming up on the side of the road. I told
her we didn't have to go home just yet. We could just pull off
the road, park the car and make out if she wanted! I felt like we
were back in school.

Noël said, "Let's do it!"

Okay, why not? I thought. Just because we were forty-eight
years old didn't mean we couldn't go parking if we wanted, did
it?

So I pulled into the state park and drove around the lake
until we found a secluded spot where we could watch the
sunset together—and kiss to our hearts' content. Like many
couples who go parking in their cars, our kisses quickly turned
into more. While kissing and caressing in every way possible
(although in a fairly cramped space, but who cares when you're
kissing the love of your life?), we both experienced a perfect
sunset. We sat and enjoyed the view for as long as we could—
both of the setting sun and of the smiles on each other's faces.

I felt like Will Turner at the end of the third *Pirates of the
Caribbean* movie, after he finally got to marry Elizabeth Swan,
the woman of his dreams. Moments after their wedding
ceremony (which took place in the midst of a fierce battle
aboard their ship), they learned that Will was going to have to
spend the rest of his life at sea, coming back to shore and
seeing his wife for only one day every ten years.

When Will's father found out what had happened, he said
to Will, "One day on shore, ten years at sea. That's a steep
price to pay for what's been done."

With a smile on his face, Will replied:

"Depends on the one day."

As tragic as Noël's imminent death might have seemed, I
was willing to go through it all again if only for just *one* of
those memorable days with her.

Depends on the one day, indeed!

Chapter 28:

Deliriously Happy

Noël had never been jealous during our entire marriage. So I was surprised when she said to me one day that summer, "I've been thinking about what would happen if I die and you get remarried. I just get so jealous thinking about it! Whoever you marry, she's going to be able to do so much more for you than I ever did, and she's going to be so much better for you than me. It just makes me so jealous!"

And Noël was totally serious.

I couldn't believe she could even think such a thing. For starters, I couldn't imagine my world without Noël in it—let alone getting remarried in that new world. If Noël were to die, which was looking more and more likely, everything beyond that point looked entirely gray—not gray like fog, just gray, blank, nothing. I couldn't picture anything in my future if Noël wasn't in it.

Second, I couldn't imagine anyone who could ever do more for me than Noël had done, from wanting to still date me after I confessed to her my homosexual attractions and then still marrying me, to helping me get comfortable in my sexual relationship with her and walking with me through countless adventures of faith when things were tough. My list of things I loved about Noël was endless. It was unimaginable to think that there could ever be anyone who was better for me than Noël.

I felt like a little boy whose parents told him that his puppy was dying, but not to worry, that they'd get him another puppy someday. I didn't *want* another puppy! I wanted *my* puppy! I didn't *want* another wife! I wanted *my* wife—Noël—forever.

I tried to tell Noël just how perfect she was for me, how much she had done for me and how much I loved her wholeheartedly, but she remained convinced that if I got married again, I would love my new wife even more.

It was a hard conversation, and it was, in a word, inconceivable! Inconceivable that I would ever get remarried and inconceivable that she really felt this way! (If someone as beautiful, talented and supremely astounding as Noël felt this way—I pitied anyone else who ever faced these questions.)

It took me a few days to try to get my head around what she was saying, what she was feeling. As much as I tried, I couldn't. I was just so sad to think about losing her. That's *all* I could think about.

As the darkness of it all began to settle over me, a new thought came into my head. *No,* I thought, *I couldn't imagine ever getting married again to another women. This was all too much work, too much effort and the pain of having it end like this hurt too much to ever do it again. But... if the right man came along...*

What?!? I thought. *Where did that thought come from?!?*

I hadn't given serious consideration to a relationship with a man for over twenty-five years. Why would I think of that now? It was just a passing thought, I knew, brought on by the pain of thinking about Noël's possible death. But still, how could I possibly picture a future with another man, when I couldn't even fathom a future with another woman?

The question plagued me the rest of that day and on into the days that followed. I couldn't get the thought out of my head. *I could never actually do it, of course (could I?).* But why did I even think about it?

I didn't have to think too hard to find an answer for that. From my perspective, a relationship with a man was all fun and games—no commitment, no responsibility, all freedom, all fun, all the time (at least that's the way I remembered it from my dating days). Still, the fact that the thought even entered my mind bothered me. I wanted to talk to someone about it, and the person I usually talked to about things like this was Noël. How could I tell her what had crossed my mind? Yet I knew she was still the best one to help me through this as well.

With prayer and a bit of hesitancy, I told her my concerns, that I couldn't imagine getting married again, but the thought did come into my mind a few days after our conversation, that if the right man (or the wrong man, as the case may be) showed up, that actually held some appeal. It scared me, I told her, and I asked if she could pray with me. She did. And two weeks later, God answered our prayers—all in the same day— in three distinct ways.

When I woke up one Sunday morning, I didn't know what to read in my Bible. So I opened at random and landed on the book of Romans. I started reading at Romans chapter one. It was the same passage I had read twenty-eight years earlier, the passage that talks about homosexuality, the passage that God had used as the turning point in my life of faith, when He put His finger on the issue of homosexuality in my life. As I read that same passage again, I felt something like light flooding back into my head, dispelling the darkness that had been hanging around like a cloud for the previous two weeks.

"That's right," I said to myself. "Jesus took my place so I could have a new life. Homosexuality is part of my past, not my present and not my future. Thank You, Lord! Thank You for reminding me what You've done in my life."

That was answer number one.

Later that morning, I went to our church and the pastor happened to be talking about homosexuality. In his message he said:

"You can argue back and forth about it all day long, but the bottom line is this: if God says something's not good for you and you do it, it's not going to go well for you."

This didn't apply just to homosexuality, he said, but to *any* topic mentioned in the Bible that God said wasn't good for us, whether it was sex before marriage or sex outside of marriage or any of the many other warnings God gives us. *If God says something's not good for you and you do it, it's not going to go well for you.* In all my years of studying this issue and hearing debates from every angle, I had never heard it expressed so clearly and simply. "If God says something's not good for you and you do it, it's not going to go well for you."

That was answer number two.

Later that same night, a friend who hadn't called in quite some time called to catch up. We had talked many times over the years about homosexuality, and we had encouraged each other in our mutual desire to leave that lifestyle behind. I mentioned to him how disturbed I was by this thought about homosexuality that had entered my head after Noël was talking about remarriage if she were to die.

My friend said, "You know, Nick, when my wife was diagnosed with cancer, I wondered the same thing, that if she died, maybe that was God's way of releasing me to go into homosexuality."

What?!? I thought. *You can't possibly mean that?!?* But he did.

You can't do that! I thought. *How crazy would that be?* But then I realized that's what I had been thinking—without the idea of doing it with God's blessing. Even though I *knew* it was wrong, I was getting to the point where I just didn't care. *If following God and following His ways only ended in losing the one person you loved most in your life, then what was the point in following Him at all?* Those were the thoughts that drifted through my head anyway.

But then I realized that it was *because* I had followed God all those years, and *because* I had received so many blessings from Him as a result, that I was now facing this heartbreak of losing one of the most precious gifts He had given me in Noël. What would have happened to me if I had pursued homosexuality and living for myself, without considering what God had in mind for me or those around me? If Noël were to die, how could I shake my fist at God say, "Why did you take her from me?" All I should be able to say would be, "Thank You, God, for giving me twenty-eight wonderful years to love this incredible woman!"

Hearing my friend on the phone speak those words out loud that I had only begun to consider in my head dealt the final blow that blasted those thoughts from my head completely. In those three answers to my prayers, all in one day, the dark clouds that had been hovering around me for two weeks straight finally dissipated *completely* from my head. I could think clearly again and had no doubt about what my future held—and it *didn't* include a relationship with a man. That final piece of darkness had fled in an instant.

In the natural world, it made sense why I would want to go back to something that had once brought me pleasure, given the fact that I might lose that which was currently bringing me pleasure. And it made even more sense in the supernatural world, where the Bible says that our struggle is not just against flesh and blood, "but against the rulers, against the authorities, against the powers of this dark world and against the spiritual forces of evil in the heavenly realms" (Ephesians 6:10-11). There *was* a battle going on in my flesh, for sure, but there was also a battle going on in the supernatural world!

Having heard so clearly from God three times in one day —once from God's Word, once from our pastor and once from a friend (in a roundabout way!), all of my doubts, fears and confusion about this issue were gone. I was able to go back to Noël and thank her for her prayers for me. God had indeed answered them!

A few months later, Noël brought up the topic of remarriage again, saying that she had thought about it more, and she was no longer jealous of whoever I might marry next

—in fact, she *hoped* I would get married again someday. Noël said I had been a great husband to her, and she knew I'd be a great husband to someone else, too.

As much as I still didn't want to think about or talk about the idea—and I still didn't see anything in my future if Noël *were* to die except gray, blank, nothingness—I couldn't help but be thankful that she had given me that blessing if I ever *did* get married again. I knew she meant it from her heart.

In a conversation between two women who had lost their husbands on the show *When Calls the Heart,* a woman named Abigail summed up what I knew Noël must have eventually wanted for me, too:

CLARA: *"Have you ever..."*

ABIGAIL: *"...opened my heart to another man? Yes. I did."*

CLARA: *"Did you feel..."*

ABIGAIL: *"...guilty? No. Because I realized, if the situation had been different, and Noah had lost me, I wouldn't have wanted him to spend the rest of his life alone. Because, when you truly love someone, all you want is for them to be happy."*

Noël truly loved me and she made me deliriously happy. While I couldn't imagine anyone else would ever be able to do the same, I knew if I *did* ever get married again, it would make Noël deliriously happy, too.

Chapter 29:

Disney Dreams

Three months after Noël's diagnosis, a friend of mine asked if my daughter and I would like to be extras in an action movie he was producing. He knew that my daughter was interested in acting, and I had told him that if he ever had a spot in a movie where he could use her to let us know.

He said the filming would be the next day in Dallas. My daughter was thrilled at the idea, so the next day we packed our bags and drove to Dallas, fourteen hours away, arriving on location at midnight, as they were shooting at night when the buildings downtown were empty.

After watching the filming of several fight scenes, our turn came up to be extras in a café scene where the lead characters were plotting their next move. It was a lot of fun as we watched how they made the movie, interacted with the cast and crew and got to be in our first Hollywood film.

While on the set, one of the production assistants heard about the story of Noël's cancer and asked if I'd be willing to do a short interview while I was there in Dallas. She said she was working on project to give hope to families facing terminal illness, and she thought people would want to hear our story.

At first, I didn't know if I could do it, as it was so hard to process all that was going on inside of me, let alone talk about it to others. Yet I wanted to help, and I didn't want to waste anything we were going through if God could do something good with it. So I said, "Yes," and the next day we met in an empty, upstairs room of a pizza place in Dallas.

I spent an hour fielding questions from this production

assistant and her colleague, which caused me to reach deep down to find whatever hope I still had left inside of me for our very bleak situation. The thought of losing Noël was constantly on my mind, and the questions the film team asked made it all the more real.

But having to search my heart for the answers to their questions, I discovered that I *did* have a lot more hope than I realized, and no matter what the future held, I knew I could trust God to work it all out for good in the end. He had already worked out so many other difficult situations in my life—in ways that I could have never imagined—so I knew I could trust Him for this, too.

At the end of the shoot, I felt better about my own situation. Somehow the answers I gave that day spoke to my own heart as well.

The resulting five-minute film captured my love for Noël in a way that I might never have been able to express otherwise. In one segment, I said:

"I heard someone say recently that Disney stories don't happen anymore—where the boy falls in love with the girl and they live happily ever after—and that we shouldn't expect that. But I can say for me and my wife, God's given us the best Disney story—just being able to be with her, be married to her, have children with her and live life with her. I know that this disease may shorten her life, but on our anniversary this year, I gave her a little plaque that said, 'And they lived happily ever after.' Even if our time is cut short here on earth together, I have no regrets. I'm so glad that I've had time to love her, and she's had time to love me. For me, it is a "happily ever after" story. Whenever love is involved, love never fails."

As I thought about those words later, I also realized that I haven't seen one Disney story yet where the main couple doesn't go through the fire, through pain and suffering and even through significant loss and death. Whether it's Cinderella going through years of hard labor and injustice before finding her prince—only to have her hopes dashed at midnight before she finally gets to live her "happily ever after"; or Will and Elizabeth in the *Pirates of the Caribbean,* fighting their way through three entire movies before they finally get married during an intense battle scene on ship—only to find out they'll be separated again for ten years for every one day they get to spend together.

Even Romeo and Juliet, in perhaps the best-known love story in the world, struggled throughout an entire Shakespearean play to spend just a few minutes together here and there—only to have it end with (spoiler alert!) their tragic deaths shortly after their one and only time to consummate their love.

No good Disney story—or any good love story for that matter—comes without trials and hardships, obstacles and heartaches, difficulties and sometimes even death. If I wanted to have the best Disney story, I was going to have to take *everything* that came along with it, including the struggles and trials along the way.

Three months after shooting that short video, Noël and I got a chance to spend an unexpected day with our three youngest kids at Disneyland in California. We had driven out west to drop our second-oldest daughter off at college in northern California, then swung down through L.A. to visit some more family and friends. We had an extra free day in L.A. before heading back home, so we decided to take our younger three kids to Disneyland.

It was a great day—but I've never prayed so much at a theme park before!

The pain in Noël's bones was increasing as the cancer was spreading throughout them, but she didn't want to miss out on one single thing. She rode every ride that the rest of us rode, from the roller coaster inside Space Mountain to the log ride at the top of Splash Mountain. One picture from that day shows all of us smiling and screaming as we plummeted down the last big drop of the log ride, with our hands in the air or covering our faces. I was smiling on the outside, but on the inside, I was praying as hard as I could that this wouldn't be the one ride that broke every bone in Noël's body!

We had rented a wheelchair for Noël to get around, because she was hardly able to walk a hundred yards without getting winded, let alone a whole day throughout the park. But that didn't stop Noël; she wanted to live every day to the fullest—and by having the wheelchair, we discovered, Noël got to go to the front of the lines, and we got to go with her!

We watched two sets of fireworks that night: one earlier in the night by the lake in Frontierland, and another later in the night on Main Street, complete with Tinker Bell flying back and forth on a zip line across the night sky, with Sleeping Beauty's castle lit up in the background. The fireworks were bursting above the castle, keeping time with the soundtrack of Disney songs and the voice-over of Julie Andrews saying, "Remember... dreams come true."

When we got back to our hotel that night, my dreams really did come true! After a dip in the pool and the hot tub with our kids, we retreated to our room—a suite where the kids had a room of their own and we had a room to ourselves, too. With visions of fireworks still in our heads, Noël and I made love and made some fireworks of our own as we laughed and kissed and touched each other under the soft white sheets of the king-sized bed. I was so thankful we had made it through the day (my prayers were answered!), and I couldn't believe I was now getting to spend a night in bed—once again—with my still-gorgeous wife after all these years.

That night turned out to be one of the most romantic, passionate and extended times of lovemaking we had ever had in our lives. I was still smiling about it so much the next morning that I had to stop and take a picture of the bed where we slept, with the sheets still rumpled and tangled from our wonderful night before.

As we drove out of the hotel parking lot that morning, I couldn't help but remember one of the dreams I had back when I was still single and living in Houston, Texas. It was the year before Noël and I were married—and we weren't even dating at the time—and I had seen a picture in a magazine of a new hotel that had just opened at Disney World in Florida, the Grand Floridian. I was so taken by that picture of the hotel that I wished I could go there someday. But not right then. Not while I was still single! I wanted to go there when I could spend a whole day riding the rides with the woman I loved, then spend the whole night making love with her in our hotel room, with visions of fireworks dancing in our heads.

After Noël and I got married, we did get to go with our kids to Disney World in Florida and Disneyland in California (although we never stayed at the Grand Floridian, as the rooms started at $500 a night!). But out of all those visits, none were as special as that night in California. It was better than I had ever pictured back when I was single, because the picture now included my sensational wife, Noël.

As I drove away from the hotel, I couldn't believe how blessed I was to get to live out my dreams with her—even my Disney dreams—spending a whole day riding the rides with the woman I loved, and spending the whole night making love with her in our hotel room, with visions of fireworks dancing in our heads.

God had given us our own special "happily ever after."

In the movie, *The Fault in Our Stars*, the main character, Hazel, who was fighting a battle with cancer, described something known as the Last Good Day, "that day when it seems like the inexorable decline has suddenly plateaued, when the pain is just for a minute bearable." She continued:

"The problem of course, is that there's no way of knowing that your last good day is your last good day. At the time, it's just another decent day."

For Noël and me, that impromptu day and night at Disneyland was extraordinary in some ways, but in terms of Noël's health, it was "just another decent day."

While Noël still had a few more "Last Good Days" after that, that day at Disneyland was one of them.

And as only God could have arranged it—knowing my long-ago dream of spending a romantic night with my beautiful wife after an adventurous day at a Disney park—that day was especially memorable for one more reason.

That was the last day we ever made love.

Chapter 30:
Last Words

The drive home from California was much harder than the drive out there, as Noël's pain was increasing exponentially throughout our trip.

We made brief stops at the Grand Canyon, where I took the kids on a short walk down the Bright Angel Trail and another stop at an Indian Reservation, where Noël delivered some gifts to a church on behalf of some friends back home. After one more stop to visit a few more friends, we pushed to get home as soon as we could, immediately setting up some appointments with Noël's various doctors to see what they could do to help.

While Noël was getting an infusion of chemotherapy and a shot to strengthen her bones, I pulled aside one of the nurse practitioners to ask her what she really thought of Noël's condition. Not wanting to scare me, but knowing that I wanted the truth, she said that based on the other patients she had seen over the years, she thought Noël might have anywhere from a few weeks to a few months left—six months at most.

A few weeks to a few months?!? What happened to "three to five years" that we thought we had just a few months earlier, the average for someone in Noël's condition? I was totally blown away. Aside from the personal shock I felt at what the nurse practitioner had just told me, I also thought of my two kids away at college, one in California and another in Australia, who weren't planning to come home until Christmas. It was only the end of September, and Christmas was still over two months away. If Noël only had a few weeks left to live, my kids in college might never get to see their mother again!

Oh, God! I thought. *I can't believe this is happening!*

The nurse cautioned me that it would be best to wait till the doctor came in on Monday morning to ask him what he thought. I appreciated her honesty, and I thought it was wise to wait to hear what the doctor said, too, before I said anything to Noël—she was facing enough already.

On Monday, we had two doctors' visits scheduled: one with her oncologist to talk about her chemo, and the other with our family doctor to talk about her pain.

After meeting with the oncologist, I pulled him aside as I had done with the nurse practitioner, this time while Noël was checking out at the front desk. I asked him about timeframes and told him about my kids being away at college until Christmas. He said, quite directly, "I'd bring them home now. At this point, her life expectancy is in weeks to months—not very long. By Christmastime, she may not even be here. You have to look at what's important, Nick. For me, there's no point in someone coming home if the person they're coming to see is in bed and can't say anything or do anything—and that's what's going to happen in a short period of time. If what's important is to be able to talk to her and be with her, then this is the time to do it. At this point, I don't think she's going to get any better."

Wanting to make sure I was hearing him right, I asked, "So the idea of another two or three years...?" I figured that three to five years was already out of the question.

"No," he said, "it's months at most. I wish I could tell you better, but I don't have a crystal ball. But I do want to be realistic with you. If she does live longer, that would be a fantastic gift—but I'm sorry, I don't think that will happen."

I thanked him for his candor, said goodbye and walked out of his office with my mind reeling. I was too numb to even think about what to tell Noël. And we still had one more doctor's visit to go.

When we met with our family doctor, he was exceptionally sympathetic, talking with Noël about her pain, prescribing some medications to help alleviate it right away and even talking with us about the spiritual aspects of our situation. Noël was so appreciative of his care, his sensitivity and his help. As the nurses walked Noël out to the lobby, I asked him if I could talk to him for just a few more minutes.

Stepping back into the room, I asked him the same thing I had asked the nurse practitioner and the oncologist regarding Noël's prognosis—and my question about bringing our kids home at Christmas.

Without even telling him what the others had said, our doctor said the same thing: "I'm sorry Nick, but I don't think she'll make it till Christmas."

He gave me some thoughts about what to do and how I might tell Noël, then I met her in the lobby and walked her to the car.

On the way home, we drove by a church we don't normally pass, as we were driving towards the pharmacy to drop off her prescription. The church had a marquee out front that said:
"Stop the search.
Drop the doubt.
Roll with the Lord."

As I read those words, I felt like God was speaking directly to my heart. Ever since Noël was first diagnosed with cancer—and the doctors thought it was still very treatable—I felt like God was telling me otherwise. In fact, God had spoken to me quite clearly. I just didn't want to believe Him.

At that time, just days after Noël was first diagnosed, she had handed me a podcast message on her phone that she thought was great, and she wanted me to listen to it. As she handed her phone to me, however, God spoke to my heart saying, "This *is* a great message, but this isn't my message for you in this situation." I was surprised to hear Him speak like that, and even more surprised when I listened to the message. It was all about asking for the moon in your prayers; not just asking to pass a class, but to pass it with an A; not just asking that your marriage would survive, but that it would thrive; not just asking for healing, but for better health than ever. It was a message that would have normally inspired me to ask for the moon—and get it. But this time was different. This time I felt God was saying to me:

"I know you could ask for the moon and get it, Nick. But not this time. This time I have something else in mind."

God then brought to my mind the words from Psalm 23:

"Even though I walk through the valley of the shadow of death, I will fear no evil, for You are with me..." (Psalm 23:4a).

Death, Lord? I thought. *Isn't that a little extreme? The doctors are saying this is totally treatable. Why would you give me a verse about death?* I hoped and prayed I had heard wrong from God on this one. *At least,* I thought, *even if this is from God, He has promised that He would be with me.*

Then, ten days later, the doctors came back with a different report, saying that Noël's cancer had already spread—and there was nothing they could do to save her.

My heart sank, but my spirit was strangely comforted. As horrific as this news was, God really *was* speaking to me. He really did know everything that was going on, and for some reason He wanted me to know even before the doctors did. God reminded me again of the words He had spoken to me before, from Psalm 23:

"Even though I walk through the valley of the shadow of death, I will fear no evil, for You are with me..." (Psalm 23:4a).

God would be with us, even through the valley of the shadow of death.

Noël didn't want to die. She wanted to live! And I wanted her to live! So we still fought for her life, sought out solutions, talked to doctors and prayed with others. But after all we had tried and all that had failed, I had to wonder if I was fighting *against* God in this, rather than with Him. When I heard three times from Noël's doctors and nurse practitioner that Noël wouldn't make it till Christmas, I felt it was time to stop the search, drop the doubt and trust that God had really spoken to me way back at the beginning of the battle when I felt He said, "I know you could ask for the moon and get it, Nick. But not this time. This time I have something else in mind."

When I saw that church sign, that was my sign!

"Stop the search.

Drop the doubt.

Roll with the Lord."

I knew I could trust God. Now I just needed the strength to tell Noël.

When we got home from the doctors appointments, Noël took off her clothes and climbed into bed. I took off mine and laid next to her under the sheets. Noël's sister had taken our kids to her house for the week so Noël could rest and we could have some time on our own.

As we lay next to each other on that Monday afternoon, with the house to ourselves and nothing but our skin between us, Noël asked me why I had stayed to talk to our family doctor after she went to the lobby. She hadn't noticed my first two conversations with the nurse practitioner and the oncologist, but she had definitely noticed the last one. She wondered what we were talking about.

"Or is it something you don't want to tell me?" she asked.

"No, I want to tell you," I said. "I just wanted to be sure."

I told her about my three conversations with her doctors and the nurse practitioner. I told her I asked them how long they thought she might have left to live. Then I told her what they said: that they thought she had only weeks or months left, not years. I told her I asked about bringing the kids home at

Christmas.

Then I said, "I'm sorry Noël, but they don't think you'll make it till Christmas."

As we lay there together, I let her digest what I was saying. Then I told her about the church sign we had both seen on the way home, and how I felt God was speaking directly to my heart, saying it was time to stop the search, drop the doubt and roll with Him. I knew there were still cancer studies and clinical trials that she wanted to try, but we had been blocked even in those at every turn. There was little else we could do, even if we wanted to.

I told her I was sorry, that I really hoped I was wrong way back at the beginning, when I felt God was speaking to me saying that we could ask for the moon and get it, but not this time, that this time God had something else in mind. But I told her that as hard as this news was, I had a deep reassurance from God that even if this *was* her time, God had already told us that we had nothing to fear. He would be with us through it all.

We talked for a few more minutes as the reality sank in for both of us. Then Noël turned to me, with her head on the pillow, and said the sweetest, most unexpected words she could have ever said to me in a moment like that. She turned to me and said:

"Let's make love."

Although she knew we couldn't, as her body was so fragile and she was in so much pain, that was what was on her heart. "I don't know how we can," she said, "but I wish we could."

We held each other close, and she put her hand on my body, in the same place where she touched me on that first day when we kissed on the beach. She would often tell me how she loved holding me there, while we were both still relaxed, and before I was aroused. It seldom lasted long, because touching me like that would usually make me go from zero to sixty in no time at all. "I love feeling you this way," she said to me again, as she had often said to me before.

This kind of touching would normally have ended up with us making love; or if she was tired or if she just wanted to please me without making love herself, she would keep touching me and stroking me until I was fully satisfied, saying that she loved putting a smile on my face—which she did.

Now here we were again, after hearing the most devastating news of our lives, lying together naked in our bed in the middle of the afternoon, and Noël had reached over and touched me there again—putting a smile back on my face again, too.

Then she drifted off to sleep, breathing quietly next to me. She was at peace. And I was at peace, soon falling asleep in her arms.

In the last few weeks that followed, Noël said many wonderful things, some of which gave encouragement and hope to thousands of people as she shared them in person and online. But the words that stuck with me the most—the words I've returned to again and again as her most precious, personal last words to me—were those that she spoke that afternoon in bed:

"Let's make love."

CONCLUSION:

Now Spoken

Six weeks after our heart-to-heart (and skin-to-skin) conversation in bed, Noël passed from this life to the next.

Our kids came home early from college and we all spent those final days with Noël, laughing and crying and holding each other close. By the time Noël was ready to draw her last breath, we were ready, too—thanks to God's early warning that Noël's life was in danger, a warning which at the time seemed like the worst news God could have ever given me. Yet in God's sovereign wisdom, He had given me another precious gift: time to plan, prepare and say goodbye properly.

Like many of the stories I've shared in this book, I've never shared those "last words" publicly until now, when Noël turned her head on the pillow and said to me, "Let's make love." Perhaps you can understand why. Some memories are too precious to be spoken out loud; doing so might shatter the special place they hold in our hearts. But some memories are too precious *not* to be spoken out loud, when doing so might bring hope and healing to the hearts of those who hear them.

That's why I've shared these stories with you now. My prayer is that, in God's unique way, He can use these stories to bring hope and healing to you—just as He's used them to bring hope and healing to me.

It's been thirty months now since Noël passed "through the veil," that thin curtain that separates heaven and earth (so thin some days that I can still practically reach out and touch her), and it's been thirty years since we first started dating with that kiss on the beach.

You may not have realized it, but this book is a collection of fifty intimate memories, fifty memories that have displayed God's grace in my life—fifty memories and fifty shades of grace. For I've found that when life gets darker, God's grace shines brighter.

So far I've shared forty-nine of those memories with you. But if I had to pick one lovemaking experience that epitomizes the redemption and freedom I felt on my journey from homosexuality to marital bliss, it would be one spectacular night with Noël at the Dead Sea which I would like to share with you now: the fiftieth and final shade of grace.

Noël and I had taken some of our kids and some of our friends on a tour of Israel, visiting places of interest throughout the country. We spent the last two nights at the Dead Sea, which turned out to be the most relaxing and memorable days of our whole trip.

I had never been to the Dead Sea before and I was expecting to see something like a swampy pond back home, full of algae and dead, smelly fish along the shore. Instead, I saw miles and miles of beautiful, crystal clear water, with a bright, blue sky up above and yellow-hued mountains all around.

There was nothing "dead" in the Dead Sea at all! There was no algae. There were no fish, no flies, no mosquitos, because nearly *nothing* had lived there for thousands of years. The high salt content of the water—more than six times the normal amount found in the world's oceans—prevented almost any kind of life from growing in the sea at all.

We had a great time with our kids and our friends, floating in the calm, warm water. And because of the high salt content, we could hardly push our bodies under the water if we tried. (And we definitely didn't put our heads under, for the water was so salty it would have stung our lips and burned our eyes.) The beauty and the mystery of that sea was amazing.

That night, after our group had gathered in Noël's and my hotel room for a time of worship and communion, thanking God for our remarkable trip, Noël and I had some time alone. We sat on the balcony overlooking the Dead Sea, which now looked cool and clam under the dark blue, nighttime sky. It was all so romantic and peaceful that instead of going to bed, we decided to bring the bed to the balcony—at least the futon mattress from the couch in the room.

Laying in each other's arms on our own private balcony— and looking up at the nighttime sky above the sea—we kissed and took off each other's clothes, piece by piece, until we were laying there perfectly naked. No one could see us over the balcony's ledge, but we could see each other, face-to-face, as well as in the reflection of the sliding glass doors that led back into the room.

I couldn't believe God had allowed me once again to lay next to the most beautiful woman on the planet, this time under the stars on a warm, fall night in an exotic locale. I praised God in my heart, and Noël with my words, for giving me yet another off-the-charts experience.

As we looked at each other, caressing each other's bodies, I couldn't help but remember that it was right there on the shores of the Dead Sea that the former cities of Sodom and Gomorrah once stood, cities which had become so wicked and vile in terms of their sexuality that God eventually destroyed them completely, raining fire and brimstone down from heaven until there was nothing left the next day but smoldering ashes.

Nothing has lived in that region ever since. No trace of those cities has ever been found. Only a few spots now show any signs of life near the Dead Sea—the spots where people have imported enough fresh water to put up a few hotels surrounded by a few trees and some green grass. Thousands of years have passed, yet the destruction of that land was so complete that it is still nearly totally barren.

It wasn't always that way, and it won't be that way forever. The Bible says that one day, when Christ returns, fresh water will again flow into the Dead Sea, coming from an underground stream in the city of Jerusalem—from the same place where Abraham once acted in faith and his son was spared; the same place where David once acted in faith and a plague was stopped; and the same place where Jesus once walked, talked and brought healing to many. From that spot, fresh water will flow into the Jordan River, all the way down to the Dead Sea, bringing life to it once again.

Fish will swim in its water and fishermen will again cast their nets from the shore. Trees, grass and vegetation of all kinds will grow along its banks.

As I laid on the balcony with Noël and thought about the miracle that will take place one day in that very same location, I couldn't help but think about the miracle God had already done in my own life when I put my faith in Jesus, His Son, bringing new life to my body and restoring me to Him—and restoring Noël and me to each other.

Because of that transformation in my life, God was now giving me, once again—right there in the middle of the desert —another Garden of Eden experience with my wife. I felt God's healing touch as Noël and I caressed each other's bodies, and I saw that touch reflected back to me in the glass doors beside us. Naked and unashamed, touching and kissing each other from head to toe, Noël and I were able to see and experience the joy of sex as God had created it, including all the arousal, the excitement, the penetration and the climax, followed by the most delightful afterglow as we both melted back down onto the futon mattress, laying completely and utterly satisfied in each other's arms.

It felt like heaven had come down to earth, and I couldn't help but feeling that God was smiling down on us as much as we were smiling at each other. God had redeemed what was lost, restored what was broken and brought healing and new life to two of His children who were once bound up and headed towards death.

As I held Noël close, still feeling the aftershocks of our mutually enjoyable, seismic experience, I couldn't help but say the same thing I said every time we made love:

"Thank You, Lord—and thank you, Noël."

And thanks for reading Fifty Shades of Grace!
To learn more, ask a question or share a comment, please visit:
WWW.NICHOLASDEERE.COM

FIFTY SHADES OF GRACE
A New Love Story for a New Millennium

Nick grew up on a typical American farm in the heart of the great Midwest. But when his best friend in college invites him into a romantic relationship, Nick's life takes an unexpected twist. Join Nick as he explores and experiences all the glorious, unpredictable and multi-faceted dimensions of a life lived in love—love with men, love with women and even love with God Himself. Filled with passion and romance, heartbreak and sex, you'll keep turning pages to find out what's next!

ABOUT THE AUTHOR

Nicholas J. Deere is the author of a weekly, inspirational message that reaches tens of thousands of readers in 160 countries. In *Fifty Shades of Grace*, Nick shares some of his most intimate, blush worthy and never-before-told stories of his own riveting life lived in love.

WHAT READERS ARE SAYING

"A gripping story—a page turner for sure!" R.E.

"Truthful and compelling. I wanted to cry and hold him and tell him everything would be alright (and sometimes box his little ears!)" J.T.

"It hooks you immediately" K.S.

"Engaging, interesting—and significant." G.P.

"Excellent! Not overly graphic, but very personal." D.M.

"A fascinating story—I think more than one wife will nudge her husband and say, 'Here. Read this.'" B.B.

"I don't think I could be so open and honest. That's probably why it is so riveting." J.L.

"A story that all of us can relate to." A.L.

44533750R00123

Made in the USA
Lexington, KY
03 September 2015